D1319818

Golf
in
Britain

Golf in Britain

A social history from the beginnings to the present day

Geoffrey Cousins

Former Golf Correspondent of the *Star*
and author of
Golfers at Law,
The Handbook of Golf,
An Atlas of Golf.

Co-author with Tom Scott of
The Wit of Golf,
The Ind Coope Book of Golf,
Golf for the Not-so-Young,
and *A Century of Opens*

Routledge & Kegan Paul
London

First published in 1975
by Routledge & Kegan Paul Ltd
Broadway House, 68–74 Carter Lane,
London EC4V 5EL
Set in 'Monotype' Baskerville type
and printed in Great Britain by
W & J Mackay Limited, Chatham

ISBN 0 7100 8028 X

Contents

Illustrations

Preface

After being a purely Scottish game for more than four centuries, golf has spread dramatically in the last hundred years and is now played throughout the world. Its adherents number many millions and are found in every clime and in all classes. The performances of star players competing for big prize-money and important titles have captured the public imagination and made golf a spectator sport with beneficial effects on its appeal as entertainment and as a pastime. Inevitably many changes have taken place in the character of the game and the attitudes of players, and a study of these developments has made it clear that social influences have always been at work in shaping present-day golf. This book is not just another history of this universal game; I have gone deeply into an analysis of how it has affected and been affected by all kinds of people over several centuries.

Fifty years of writing on this subject has eased my task, because research has taken me along well-trodden paths and into familiar territory, although I have often stepped aside to discover fresh aspects. There have also been many helpful guides along the way. My thanks are due first to my old friend George Gibson for giving me permission to browse through his extensive library of old golf books, and to Mr Marshall Lumsden, the present managing director of the Professional Golfers' Co-operative Association, for providing the necessary facilities. Mr George McPartlin, Secretary of the Golf Development Council and of Golf Foundation Ltd, has kept me up to date with progress in both those enterprising bodies; and has also helped me to delve into the early history of the London Scottish Golf Club. Mr W. (Bill) Farley, Honorary Secretary of the Artisan Golfers' Association, has been of equally valuable assistance in that field. My researches into the early history of ladies' golf in Scotland would have been very difficult but for the help of Mrs R. B. How of the St Rule Golf Club, and of Miss Christo Douglas of the Ladies' Putting Club of St Andrews, both of whom so kindly provided me with copies of relevant documents. I am also grateful to my friend and erstwhile colleague Miss Enid Wilson, women's golf correspondent of the *Daily Telegraph* for her guidance on the history of the Girls' Championship.

Mr E. G. Bourne-Vanneck of the National Association of Public Golf Courses; the late Mr C. K. Cotton, Association of British Golf Architects; Mr Patrick Smartt the historian of Sussex golf; my very old friend Captain Gerald Openshaw, former Secretary of Royal Wimbledon; to all these, as well as to many golf club secretaries and individuals in various quarters, who so obligingly answered my queries and offered information, my thanks are due.

CHAPTER I

Scottish beginnings— free for all

Golf began so long ago that no investigation takes us back further than the fourteenth and fifteenth centuries, when it was popular with all classes at various places in east Scotland. It was then a simple game with simple implements, often improvised. The playing areas were called links—a term for undulating and rough sandy terrain near the seashore, open to all inhabitants and used also for grazing cattle, breeding rabbits, drying clothes and practising archery and other military exercises. The links were playgrounds for children, dallying-places for lovers, promenades for sober citizens—all things to all men in their seasons. Golf in those times was a game for the people with few, if any, class distinctions. It is so today, but during the seventeenth and eighteenth centuries and for a great part of the nineteenth the sharp distinctions between classes, existing in society as a whole, were marked almost as clearly among golfers.

One of the principal reasons was that, from being a simple, almost primitive game it had become expensive in time and money, due largely to the development of clubs and balls which, being produced by craftsmen, commanded high prices. The upper classes could afford to play frequently and in a sophisticated way. The lower classes were not forced to abstain, but they had to proceed on comparatively modest lines, and this created contrasts which became stronger as development continued. Distinctions of that kind, sustained from Stuart days to the mid-Victorian epoch, are now blurred almost beyond recognition. Those that survive in an emphatic form do so by tacit mutual tolerance and arouse neither comment nor rancour.

The sparse records of golf in the fifteenth century provide a charming picture of the simple life. Everyone from little boys to dignified elders played on the same strip of ground, each in his own way and according to his means. There were no charges for the use of the links, no rules, no specified designs for clubs and balls, as there are today. The barefoot bairn with a bent stick from the hedgerow and any missile he could find was as much a user of the links as the merchant or nobleman with a stock of expensive balls and a caddie to carry his clubs. No doubt if the laddie got in the way he was cuffed and told to make himself scarce, but nothing could stop him becoming a golfer.

Yet even then the halcyon days were numbered, for the earliest historical reference to golf indicated restraint of freedom. In 1457 the youthful James II of Scotland, whose councillors disapproved of citizens spending their leisure time playing golf and football to the neglect of training for archery in preparation to fight the English, signed an edict banning both sports and requiring regular attendance at the butts. Football and golf were described as 'un-profitable sports' which were to be 'utterly cryit doun and not usit', but the edict affected only the citizenry. Nobles and lairds continued to play, and this was the first sharp division between the classes.

When Scotland and England patched up their differences in 1503 for a short and uneasy period there was no need to proscribe golf, although it was still an offence to play on Sundays 'in time of sermons'. By then the game was becoming standardized. It was no longer a haphazard exercise with sticks and stones, but a pastime with recognized implements. The accounts of the royal treasurers of the time make frequent references to the purchase of clubs and balls for the king's sport, so such articles were being produced by craftsmen according to traditional designs and methods. The ball in general use for at least five hundred years to the middle of the nineteenth century was made from a leather bag stuffed with feathers, and there is no record of any alternative during that time, except of course for various improvisations by individuals. The case was made by cutting pieces of cowhide, stitching them together except for one seam and turning them inside out to form a roughly spherical bag. The open seam was partly closed and the feathers pushed through the narrow opening left. This part of the operation, slow and difficult, was the most important factor in producing a ball which would be hard yet resilient and capable of fairly accurate flight. As many feathers as would fill a top hat were required for each ball and, having been boiled to make them manageable, they were thrust into the bag by various tools. The final ramming, done with a wooden peg attached to a breastplate strapped across the workman's breast, was exhausting and dangerous to health, because of the pressure on the chest and the inhaling of feather dust. The finished ball was hammered to make it as round as possible, and painted. Known as a 'featherie' it was by no means ideally suited to its purpose, being unpredictable in behaviour and of doubtful durability. In wet weather it became heavier and sluggish, and it could be cut and ruined by a mis-hit with an iron club or contact with a sharp stone. The loss of a ball was a serious matter, for it could cost four or five shillings, or a week's pay for an artisan.

Good workmanship and sound materials were therefore of prime importance, and the most efficient ball-makers were renowned wherever golf was played. The earliest to be named was James Melville, who in 1618 received the grant of a monopoly from James I. He had partners and assistants and could lease his rights to other makers, but every ball produced had to bear his stamp and he was authorized to 'seek out and confiscate' illegal ones. In 1642, after the Melville monopoly had expired, John Dickson of Leith was appointed by Aberdeen Town Council to make and sell balls in that district, and during the next hundred and fifty years the number of craftsmen increased as golf itself spread to different parts of the kingdom. In the last golden years of the 'featherie'—the first half of the nineteenth century—the foremost makers were John Gourlay of Musselburgh and Allan Robertson of St Andrews, the latter being associated with Tom Morris senior.

If the quality of a ball depended on the skill of the maker, this was no less true of the club-making art, which was brought to a high pitch by several craftsmen in the late eighteenth and early nineteenth century. Originally one club, rude in design and work-manship, sufficed for all shots. As the game developed, clubs were made for different kinds of stroke, but for a long time they were made entirely of wood, the shafts usually of ash and the heads of thorn or some similar hard material. The first clubs with iron heads were made primarily for use when the ball lay in a depression or a rut from which it could not be dislodged with a wooden club, and these irons could obviously not have been usable for straightfor-ward shots. Eventually they were designed for hitting the ball from flat ground when a high trajectory was required to send it over an obstacle, or for approaching the hole from a short distance. The shaft for both wood and iron clubs was rounded and tapered to provide the requisite amount of flexibility without weakness. A wooden club was made by shaping a piece of hard wood to provide a striking head with an upturned neck, to which the thinner end of the shaft was attached. The neck of the head was bevelled and the 'scare', as it was called, was glued to a similar bevel on the shaft, the joint being bound with twine. Iron heads were forged by hand and had a hollow neck, called a pipe, into which the shaft end was pushed and secured by a rivet.

The clubs used rarely numbered more than five or six, even in the case of well-to-do players, and they were carried by a caddie in the crook of his arm. Caddie bags were not introduced until about 1880. The caddie had the additional task of running forward, after handing the required club to the player, to watch the flight of the ball and spot where it landed. Without this precaution the ball could easily be lost in the rough country and sandy wastes of the links. Citizens of the poorer class could not afford caddies, and this was only one of the economic factors which contributed to a widening division between the classes. The high cost of balls, due mainly to the time spent in manufacture—the best workman could produce only three or four in a day—and the development of clubs from single all-purpose instruments to sets of specialized variety, brought the game more and more under the control of those who could afford expensive equipment and had the leisure time in which to use it. Everybody continued to play on the links but there were tacitly accepted distinctions. The gentlemen became exclusive, the artisans and tradesmen knew their places, and a third class, composed of club- and ball-makers, caddies and professional players, made golf their livelihood.

The situation developed gradually during the eighteenth century and took golf and golfers away from the primitive and unsophisticated conditions of earlier times. Although many theories about the origins of the game have been advanced, no tangible evidence exists earlier than the first proscriptive edict of 1457. Whether it was indigenous to Scotland or an adaptation of one of several club-and-ball games played in Holland, Belgium and France is and always will be a matter for conjecture and argument, although the fact that the early golf links were all on the east coast, close to ports connected with the Continental trade, is not without significance. Little is known about those times because there was no organized golf till the eighteenth century and therefore there were no records. Golfers met on the links, arranged matches and played for stakes in kind or in cash, but each match was a separate entity. It was natural for golfers of the same class and with similar occupations and inclinations to segregate themselves, but whereas the humble citizen had to play in whatever spare time he could afford, golfers of the leisured class were able to indulge in the habit of meeting on specified days for matches. The programme of 'match day' was completed by eating and drinking together, discussing the matches just played and making wagers on matches to come. That they also held inquests on the day's play and passed judgment on disputed points cannot be doubted. All this added considerably to their prestige on the links. The lairds, the landed gentry, lawyers, clergymen, doctors, professors and officers were well qualified by birth, education and circumstances to be accorded not only priority when playing golf, but also deference to their decisions affecting play.

Such was the life of golfers for many years before the formation of societies or clubs, which were instituted in the eighteenth century to meet the need for some more comprehensive form of competition than the man-to-man match, which had no connection with any other game in progress at the same time. From the earliest days there was rivalry on the links, for the game by its very nature lacks interest unless one side is pitted against another. Until nearly the middle of the eighteenth century the only known form of contest was the match. Nowadays match-play competitions are limited to those which must be decided on knock-out or league principles, and nearly all the major world events are decided by stroke play, in which the total of strokes played in a round or several rounds determines the issue. Most club competitions are also played by strokes, either as complete round scores or against the bogey or par scores of the holes. The par score is the number of strokes which should be expended at a given hole by a player of championship class. The bogey score in Britain is usually one or two strokes easier than par for the whole round, to suit the handicap player, but in the United States 'bogey' means a score of one over par for the hole.

Two hundred years ago the stroke competition was a novelty. Bogey was not introduced until 1891, and par is of still later date. All golf competitions prior to about 1760 were by matches, and the result depended not on the total of strokes for the round but on the number of holes won by a side. The links and commons in Scotland were rough, unkempt areas, used for many purposes besides golf, and remaining much as nature made them. The crude equipment, the difficulty of the hazards and the inexorable rule that the ball had to be played where it lay, combined to make every hole an adventure, the issue depending as much on the misfortunes of the loser as on the prowess of the winner. If the ball could not be recovered from a bad place, or were lost, the hole had to be surrendered; and if it could be extricated only after several strokes, the situation of the luckless player was no better, since an indifferent score by his opponent would still win the hole. But only that hole was involved, the strokes taken were not recorded, even if they were counted at all, and the loser of the hole could start from the next tee with a chance of retrieving the situation. So matches were by holes and usually by 'holes up', the full round being played and the winner counting the number of holes by which he led at the finish. By modern usage the match is over when the leader is more holes up than remain to be played; for example, a player six up after thirteen holes would be the winner by six and five (six up and five to play). Under the 'holes up' system, a player six down at the same point could win the remaining five holes and so lose only by one. This method made it possible to compare one player's performance with that of others in separate matches; and when team contests began, they were decided by 'holes up' until very recent times.

In the early eighteenth century golfers had become so accustomed to meeting for separate matches on regular occasions that they felt the need for a competition in which all could take part. In March 1744, the gentlemen who frequented Leith links asked the Edinburgh councillors to furnish a prize, and on 7 March an Act of Council authorized the city treasurer to arrange for a silver club to be made, not exceeding fifteen pounds sterling in value, to be played for annually on the first Monday in April. This move was in response to representations by 'several Gentlemen of Honour, skilful in the ancient and healthfull exercise of the Goff', and the council also approved of conditions drawn up for the event. These provided for all entry fees (at five shillings sterling for each player) to be at the disposal of the winner, who was required to attach a gold or silver piece to the club, and would be 'Captain of the Goff' for the ensuing year. Subsequently the minute book of this society of Gentlemen Golfers (now the Honourable Company of Edinburgh Golfers) had this record:

Leith, April 2, 1744: The Silver Club having been played for, Mr. John Rattray, Surgeon in Edinburgh, is declared to have won the same; in witness thereof the whole players are hereunto subscribing (Hew Dalrymple, Geo. Suttie, Ja. Leslie, Ja. Carmichael, Richd. Cockburn, Robert Biggar, Dav. Dalrymple, James Gordon.).

The conditions approved by Edinburgh Council covered only the organization of the competition, and it was necessary to ensure that all competitors had official guidance for dealing with problems which might be encountered during play. The local golfers knew by usage what procedure to adopt in various contingencies. But the event was not confined to them, and any stranger who entered would be at a loss without some written instructions. The original conditions provided for the competitors being sent out in pairs or 'by threes if their number be great'. Furthermore it was laid down that the player winning the greatest number of holes would be the winner. Clearly, therefore, they played a series of matches on the same day and John Rattray won because he finished more 'holes up' than anyone else. The material fact was that the contest involved players competing not only with their immediate rivals but also against all other entrants, and some form of control was required to ensure that all played and behaved according to accepted regulations. So the Gentlemen Golfers of Edinburgh drew up thirteen rules, the first to be put down on paper. They were simple and uncomplicated, and some would qualify today only as 'local rules' applying to a particular course. But they were adopted almost word for word by St Andrews golfers ten years afterwards, and represented the start of organized golf.

The Royal and Ancient Golf Club of St Andrews, ruling body of British golf, dates from that competition held in 1754, but the links of St Andrews had then been in use for more than three hundred years. St Andrews University, the first in Scotland, was founded in 1412, and the importance of the place was emphasized when Bishop Kennedy of St Andrews became Regent of Scotland during the minority of James III, who succeeded to the throne as an infant three years after his father had signed the first edict against golf. But the first documentary evidence of St Andrews golf is dated 1552, when the City Council licensed John Hamilton, Archbishop of St Andrews, to preserve rabbits within the northern part of the common links adjoining the Water of Eden. The rabbit-keeping activities were not to affect the community's right to 'play at golf, football, archery, all games and all other pastimes, as anyone pleases'. Nearly two hundred years later another licence for preserving rabbits stipulated that the links 'are not to be spoiled where the golfing is used'. The inescapable inference is that by the early eighteenth century golf had become important enough to be given preference over other games and activities. Although the links remained common land, the fact that practically every male citizen of St Andrews was a golfer, as well as were most of the local worthies, ensured respect for those parts where golf was played. The northern portion referred to in the 1552 deed must have embraced most of the land on which the Old Course is laid out, because the green at the short eleventh, farthest point from the city, is on the banks of the Eden River. The inhabitants of St Andrews mixed golf with other amusements for generations until golf became the paramount activity and the way was clear for the game to become organized. The crucial step was taken by the lairds and gentlemen who, in this matter as in others, took an initiative which the citizenry followed.

The Earl of Elgin and Lord Wemyss were among the twenty-two who met on 14 May 1754, to draft rules and arrange a competition, open 'to all in the British Isles', for a silver club. The two actions were interconnected. It would have been impossible to hold a competition for players from all parts, some of whom might be unfamiliar with local conditions, without ensuring that everyone played according to the same regulations. The significance of this meeting, promoted by 'The Society of Golfers of St Andrews', was that it was the work of noblemen and gentlemen, just as the decision to start a competition at Leith was taken by the gentlemen golfers of Edinburgh. Many of the twenty-two St Andrews pioneers also played at Leith, and some Leith golfers competed for the St Andrews silver club. The fact that the Leith rules were adopted for St Andrews indicates a close liaison between the two places, as far as golf among the upper classes was concerned. This is not to say that only the upper classes were capable of organization, which was not needed for golf itself, since there was no question of priority for anyone on links free for all. The gentlemen of Edinburgh and St Andrews embodied themselves to hold competitions, and in doing so automatically and unwittingly made themselves superior to other users of the links.

Different circumstances surrounded the early days of the Edinburgh Burgess Golfing Society (now Royal Burgess Golfing Society of Edinburgh), the founders of which played on the Brunts Field, a piece of land forming part of the Burgh Muir. In the eighteenth century it was an open space used by all the inhabitants for all purposes. There the burgesses and citizens of the capital played golf and eventually formed themselves into two clubs—the Burgess Society and the Bruntsfield Links Golf Club, claiming as their respective foundation dates 1735 and 1761. It is now generally assumed, because so many of the early clubs began haphazardly and often developed from loose associations of friends, that the foundation year for each should be that of the first competition or the first minutes. By this calculation the two dates mentioned should be 1773 for the Edinburgh Burgess Society and 1787 for the Bruntsfield Links club, but the earlier dates claimed cannot be contested. It is obvious that golf was being played on the Brunts Field for many years even before 1735.

The early membership of the Burgess Society was so varied as to suggest a rather more democratic atmosphere than in the case of the Honourable Company and the St Andrews Society. Nearly half the members were lawyers, but the others represented many different occupations. There were three architects and five bankers, together with bakers, goldsmiths, glaziers, grocers, hairdressers, masons and ropemakers.

The Brunts Field eventually became too inconvenient for golf. Both clubs moved to Musselburgh and eventually, towards the end of the nineteenth century, to their present quarters in the Barnton district of Edinburgh. The Royal Musselburgh club, which dates from 1774, also moved eventually to a private course at Prestonpans. Among other early clubs were those established at Aberdeen (1780), Crail (1786), Glasgow (1787), Dunbar (1794) and Burntisland (1797). Most of these were on the east coast of Scotland, and the stream of development moved sluggishly at first. But by the middle of the nineteenth century, when Prestwick was started on the west coast, it was flowing swiftly, soon to become a flood.

When the gentlemen golfers of Edinburgh and St Andrews took the first steps towards corporate existence, they consolidated the superior position they already occupied among other users of the links by virtue of class. Although both the competitions they started were open to all, they were restricted to entrants who were socially acceptable. However free from class distinctions golf might have been in earlier times, the institution of competitions and the drafting of rules, which gave the rule-makers added power, created a clear distinction between those who were organized and therefore strong, and those who were unorganized and therefore weak.

CHAPTER 2

Towards social exclusiveness

Two other factors in the growing exclusiveness of the superior classes were the introduction of club uniforms and the use of private quarters for social purposes, both intended to alleviate to some extent the disadvantages of golf on public links. The St Andrews gentlemen had less cause for complaint than their friends in Edinburgh, for the links of Leith was always uncomfortably crowded. There were only five holes, and the space available was used by many others besides golfers. These difficulties at St Andrews were borne more easily because the Old Course holes were not huddled together but strung along the seashore away from the city. (An early view of the links is reproduced in Plate 1.) When the St Andrews golfers had traversed the first hole or two they had the field more or less to themselves. But the area close to the residential part must often have been difficult to negotiate. The nearby Swilcan Burn was used for washing clothes, the clean linen being spread on the surrounding turf to dry. In 1851 one of the new rules made for St Andrews links stated: 'When a ball is on clothes or within a club-length of a washing-tub the clothes may be drawn from under the ball and the tub may be removed.' This rule was changed in 1888 to read: 'When a ball lies on clothes the ball may be lifted and dropped behind without penalty.' Whatever the reason for the change, it is clear that even in the 1880s St Andrews golfers had to contend with other users of the links.

Indiscriminate use of the playing space by many people for many purposes could not be prevented—the links were free, and the most upper-class golfers could expect was some degree of priority springing from the respect of others for their affluence and standing. So the first efforts at exclusiveness concerned the provision of quarters where they could enjoy privacy off the course.

The Gentlemen of Edinburgh began to dine after play in a private room in Lucky Clephan's Inn. Members of the Edinburgh Burgess Society adjourned from Bruntsfield Links to Maggie Johnson's. At St Andrews the first quarters of the future Royal and Ancient Golf Club seemed to be any place where they could gather. For a long time they were accustomed to meeting once a fortnight for a round and afterwards going to the house of Baillie Glass, to dine at one shilling a head. Later other places of call were used, but not until 1835, shortly after the Society had assumed its present title, did the members have a settled meeting-place. Then an amalgamation with the Union Club, with headquarters in the Union Parlour, gave them a regular home which served till the present clubhouse was built in 1852.

The fashion for uniforms in the eighteenth century was not confined to golfers, but they had a need to be marked apart from others on the links, and most of the early clubs introduced uniform coats for this purpose. They also had rigid rules requiring members to wear uniform at club meetings and dinners, under penalty. In 1787 members of the Honourable Company were shown a uniform coat designed by an Edinburgh tailor and requested to appear in that dress 'as soon as they conveniently can'. Six months later it was decreed that every member must dine in his uniform at every public meeting of the club and wear it when playing golf. Several cases of penalties were recorded and even fifty years later, according to a minute of 1837, Mr John Wood was fined 'two tappit hens' for appearing on the links without his red coat.

At St Andrews in 1780 the Society members agreed on a club jacket of red with yellow buttons, and a uniform 'frock' of buff, with a red cap. In 1790 the Edinburgh Burgess golfers adopted a scarlet jacket with a black collar, bearing a club badge. Red was not the universal colour. Glasgow golfers were obliged to wear a grey jacket or be fined a bottle of rum; and there were cases of green coats with scarlet facings, and other colour combinations. Red was considered the most useful colour as it showed up well against green and sandy surroundings; conversely green must have been most unsuitable. Today the only places where the wearing of red coats is compulsory are certain public links on common land, including Wimbledon and Chingford, where it is necessary to warn other users of the presence of golfers and therefore the risk of being struck by a ball. The red tail coat with facings is still to be seen on formal occasions, when worn by past and present captains at club dinners. This exotic reminder of the eighteenth century is seen *en masse* when members of the various Societies of Golf Club Captains dine together.

In the early years of those ancient societies the wearing of uniforms and the use of private clubrooms did little to alleviate the discomfort of playing on crowded links. Even Lucky Clephan's, where the Gentlemen of Edinburgh had a room, was an inn used by others. That particular difficulty was overcome in 1768 when they built their own clubhouse at the south-western corner of Leith links; but the problem of elbow-room on the course was not solved, and then only for a time, until they deserted Leith for Musselburgh in 1836. Musselburgh, although further from Edinburgh, had nine holes against five. When the Honourable Company moved there they at first had quarters in another inn—McKendrick's—and later found better accommodation in the grandstand of the race-course, which occupied the same ground. Another half-century passed in increasing difficulties, for the nine holes of Musselburgh became just as impossibly overcrowded as those at Leith. Again the Honourable Company needed to move, and this time were determined to secure for themselves and their visitors that exclusiveness which could never be enjoyed on a public links. They obtained a stretch of land between Gullane and North Berwick and there, in 1891, laid out the Muirfield links which, in its present form, has proved to be one of the finest on the Open Championship list.

By that time the Firth of Forth coast east of Edinburgh had become a treasure-land of golf, with great links stretching from Musselburgh to North Berwick and, beyond, to Dunbar. The original Muirfield, laid out on ground bordering Archerfield Wood, compared unfavourably with its near neighbours, since the ground was marshy in parts and rather flat. Many years later in 1924, the Honourable Company secured another piece of land nearer the seashore, adjacent to their original property, and so were enabled to extend the course and bring it to its present excellence. But in 1891 the members were not disposed to cavil at any shortcomings in the quality of their new home. They had achieved privacy.

CHAPTER 3

Early golf in England to 1800

Although Englishmen did not take up golf until the middle of the nineteenth century, it was introduced to England soon after the accession of James I (James VI of Scotland) following the death of Elizabeth I in 1603. James and his courtiers played over Blackheath in 1608, when the Court was at Greenwich, but this date has no significance in the history of the Royal Blackheath Golf Club which, according to the first recorded minutes, was formed in 1787. Clubs of any kind were unknown in early Stuart times, but it is not improbable that the heath itself was used for golf for many years before that date. At one time a desolate spot, it became a popular place for public recreation, with the development of London suburbs and the growth of population, and eventually the Royal Blackheath club moved to a private course at Eltham, thus following the example of the Honourable Company.

There is no clue at all to the time when play began on other London open spaces such as Wimbledon, Clapham, Mitcham, Tooting Bec and Chingford, but it is known that a golfing ground existed at Molesey Hurst, on the Surrey bank of the Thames, in the eighteenth century. In 1758 three Scots played there at the invitation of David Garrick, the actor-manager, who lived on the opposite bank of the river. The Rev. Alexander Carlyle, known as Jupiter Carlyle and one of the leaders of the moderate party in the Scottish Church, had come to London with another clergyman and the playwright-preacher John Home, in connection with the production of Home's play *Douglas* at Covent Garden, with Peg Woffington as leading lady.

Carlyle wrote in his autobiography (quoted by Robert Clark in *Golf: A Royal and Ancient Game*, page 23):

Garrick told us to bring golf clubs and balls that we might play
at the golf on Molesly [*sic*] Hurst. We accordingly set out in good
time, six of us in a landau. As we passed through Kensington the
Coldstream Regiment were changing guard, and on seeing our
clubs they gave us three cheers in honour of a diversion peculiar
to Scotland. . . . Garrick met us by the way, so impatient he
seemed to be for his company. Immediately after we arrived we
crossed the river to the golfing ground, which was very good.
None of the company could play but Home and myself and Parson
Black. . . . After dinner Garrick ordered the wine to be carried to
a temple in the garden. Having observed a green mount opposite
the archway, I said to our landlord that I would surprise him with
a stroke at the golf, as I should drive a ball through his archway
into the Thames, once in three strokes. I had measured the
distance with my eye in walking about the garden and
accordingly, at the second stroke, made the ball alight in the
mouth of the gateway and roll down the green slope into the
river. This was so dexterous that he was quite surprised, and
begged the club of me by which such a feat had been performed.

The temple can still be seen on the left of the Hampton Court–
Staines road near Hampton village, but the 'golfing ground' on the
other side of the river is no more. It was probably in continuous use
for at least two centuries, and eventually became a proper golf
course when the Molesey Hurst club was formed in 1907. But the
builders stepped in during the 1930s and that was the end of golf
on the Hurst, a stretch of riverside meadow which for generations
had been used for golf, football, quoits, wrestling, foot-racing and
horse-racing—the general fun of village life on high days and
holidays. Probably the last connection with the old times was the
Hurst Park racecourse, and that, too, disappeared after the Second
World War.

Dr Carlyle's account suggests that, although golf was known in
England at that time, it was played almost exclusively by Scots.
Only three in his party played and they were all Scottish. Garrick
did not play, nor his other guests. The astonishment at Carlyle's
pitch shot indicated a general ignorance among the non-players of
the technique involved. Dr Carlyle referred to the cheers of the
Coldstream Guards for 'a diversion peculiar to Scotland'. Since
they were asked to bring clubs and balls to Hampton, their host
must have known they had brought their gear from Scotland in the
expectation of playing somewhere in London. Apart from Molesey
Hurst they could have played, and probably did, on Blackheath or

Wimbledon Common or any one of several other open spaces in and around London.

They might have gone further afield, to Brighton, for instance, where it is probable that golf was played early in the nineteenth century, if not before. Patrick Smartt, whose investigations into the history of Sussex clubs have yielded many interesting facts, refers to a quatrain written on the fly-leaf of a book published in 1793, the third and last edition of Thomas Mathison's well-known poem on *The Goff* which introduced many of the early members of the Honourable Company. This particular volume, once in the library of the Royal Blackheath club but since lost, contained the following added lines, unsigned and undated:

> From London some sons of Auld Reekie set forth
> To establish at Brighton a wee club of goff;
> The green at Blackheath is indeed very fair,
> But Blackheath with Brighton can never compare.

These lines could have been scribbled in the book at any time after 1793, but circumstances and the use of the archaic spelling of golf suggest that it was not long afterwards. In 1783 the Prince of Wales, the future George IV, paid his first visit to Brighton, which remained his favourite resort for nearly half a century. His influence was responsible for the Royal Pavilion and the rest of the Regency buildings and squares which give Brighton its individual look. In the middle of the eighteenth century Richard Russell, advocating the medicinal virtues of seawater, settled in Brighton to test his theories. This began the craze for sea-bathing, and the first royal visit may well have been to assess the claims being made for 'Dr Brighton'. The continued enthusiasm of the Prince of Wales inevitably attracted society to a resort so easily reached from London, and among the many who found it fashionable and beneficial to go to Brighton there must have been some acquainted with golf. It is not impossible that the Prince Regent played, for in 1834 his brother, when William IV, became patron of the Society of St Andrews Golfers, and authorized the change of name to The Royal and Ancient Golf Club of St Andrews. The king's interest could have sprung from practical experience; on the other hand, as Duke of St Andrews, he might have thought it politic to take some notice of a pastime for which that city was famous.

There is no ground for the assumption that golf was played continuously in England from the accession of James I onwards—even by Scots. There were troublous times, including the Civil Wars with their puritanical influences; and the regime of William and Mary must have been almost equally discouraging to frivolity and sporting activities. Nevertheless, it is not without significance that there was a golfing ground at Molesey Hurst, very close to Hampton Court Palace, which William III preferred to Whitehall. He must have been well acquainted with the Dutch games played on ice and in enclosed courts, and if the courtiers of James I played at Blackheath it is not unreasonable to suppose that those of William and Mary played on Molesey Hurst. With all these facts and fancies in mind we cannot be sure that no Englishman played golf in the eighteenth century, but the nineteenth was more than half over before the first definite move was made to establish English golf, as distinct from Scottish golf, in England.

CHAPTER 4

The first 'English' clubs

For many years after the accession of James I most of the Scots who settled in England went to London, the centre of government, their activities being concerned mainly with the Court. But by the beginning of the nineteenth century Scots had considerable stakes in the business and industrial life of the country, and firms in Glasgow, Edinburgh, Aberdeen and other cities were establishing branches across the Border. One of the obvious places was Manchester, a thriving city second only to London in importance and more conveniently placed in those days of slow and difficult travel. The Scots who went to work in Manchester soon saw the possibilities for golf on the moors near by, and were mainly responsible for starting the Old Manchester Golf Club, founded in 1818 on the slopes of Kersal Edge. It is unlikely that these activities created much interest among the locals, and although in time the membership became distinctly English in character and contributed to the spread of golf in the north of England, the process was gradual. Although it cannot be denied that the Old Manchester was the second club to be formed in England, junior only to the Royal Blackheath, the distinction of being the first 'English' club belongs to the Royal North Devon, founded at Westward Ho! in 1864. Another claim, which cannot be contested, is that the Royal North Devon is the oldest club in England still using the original ground. The members play over Northam Burrows where they started, whereas the original Blackheath and Old Manchester courses have long since ceased to be used for golf.

All the founders of the Royal North Devon club were local residents, scarcely any of whom had had any experience of golf. But that is not to say that Scotland had nothing to do with the case. The Vicar of Northam, the village overlooking the links, had a sister married to General George Moncrieff, who lived in St Andrews. Many years before he went to Northam, the Rev. I. H. Gossett paid visits to St Andrews, where he must have seen golfers in action and possibly played himself. Another sister was married to an Army officer stationed at Ayr who became a keen player on the neighbouring Prestwick links. In 1853 the vicar was visited by General Moncrieff, who, walking on Northam Burrows with his host, uttered that oft-quoted remark: 'Providence evidently intended this for a golf links.' His enthusiasm was contagious, and soon the vicar and his neighbours were getting clubs and knocking balls along the cattle-grazed patches between masses of rushes. Mr Gossett, recalling his early experiences at St Andrews, taught his three sons, and soon a course of some kind developed on the rough land lying between Northam on its hill and the Pebble Ridge which protects the Burrows from the sea.

The years went by without any attempt at organization, but in 1860 Tom Morris, then professional and greenkeeper at Prestwick, was invited, probably on the recommendation of the officer at Ayr, to convert the haphazard lay-out into a proper course. From that to the formation of a club was but a matter of time. To overcome the inconvenience of transporting their clubs and other equipment from their homes each time they played, the golfers rented a room in a farmhouse near the course; and there, early in 1864, they reached a decision. The club officially came into existence on 4 April at a meeting in Bideford, the notice claiming that Northam Burrows was one of the few places in Britain suitable for golf, an assertion based on local pride rather than worldly experience. The chosen name was 'The North Devon and West of England Golf Club', and this was changed in 1867, when the Prince of Wales became patron, to 'Royal North Devon'. The first President was the Hon. Mark Rolle, the first secretary and treasurer the Rev. Lymbear Harding, and the first Captain Mr Gossett, who had started it all.

One of the founder members was Colonel George Hutchinson, whose son Horace was a member of Oxford University Golf Club, started in 1875. Later he won the Amateur Championship twice and became a prolific writer on golf and other subjects. He had clear memories of what golf was like on Northam Burrows in the early years, when the only expense was for clubs and balls. The sheep and cattle cropped the grass, and holes were made in the greens by cutting the turf with a clasp-knife round a jampot, and scooping out the sandy soil. The contentment of the pioneers with these primitive conditions was such that some eyebrows were raised when a hole-cutting tool was acquired from St Andrews.

The first 'clubhouse' was a bathing-machine which, on competition days, was stocked with food and drink and dragged to the course by coastguards. In sequence a bell tent, a marquee, and a wooden hut with a tin roof served the same purpose in progressive degrees of luxury. The hut was pitched on the edge of the Pebble Ridge because the 'pot-wallopers', as the local cattle owners were called, resented any intrusion on their right to graze the Burrows. Even when a bad Atlantic storm sent breakers over the Ridge and flooded the hut, it could be moved only to a more sheltered spot still close to the shore. The hut was big enough to hold a rough table, some forms for seating, and a bench for the bar. The members kept their clubs and other gear on the rafters.

The rough-cut holes grew larger as the day's play progressed and became notched and roughened at the edges, so for the later players the advantage of putting into a wider hole must have been nullified by the worn surface around it. There was no fixed plan for cutting new holes, and if a player found one too much damaged he would just cut another which would be used by all the following players. The site would be marked by a seabird's feather stuck in the ground near by. The first permanent clubhouse built in 1887 was heralded as a thing of beauty, attractive and commodious. Built of wood and iron it contained a saloon 50 ft by 25 ft, two dressing-rooms each 20 ft by 15 ft, a committee room, a bar, and a drying-room, the whole costing £800.

Although the club by then was nearly a quarter of a century old, the members still had modest ideas about amenities, and this could be said of most clubs starting during the next decade or so, until sophisticated attitudes were adopted as golf became popular. But in 1887 golf in England was played by only a few people, all belonging to the upper classes, and was regarded with indifference, if not with suspicion and aversion, by the uninitiated majority. The locals of Westward Ho!, accustomed to their cattle and sheep wandering everywhere on the Burrows, were naturally opposed to the use of the ground for other purposes. The early days of the club were disturbed by much animosity on the part of the pot-wallopers, extending at times to the damaging of holes and greens; and at one stage the villagers met in Northam to debate whether golf should be allowed to continue on the Burrows. This move failed, and it may be assumed that most of the responsible villagers were aware that golf would increase the prosperity of the neighbourhood. Some of them were employed by the golfers and most of the boys and young men worked as caddies in their spare time. So the critical stage passed and in 1895 the Royal North Devon Golf Club acquired the Manor of Northam, thus gaining control, through trustees, over the land. At about the same time a Burrows Committee was formed by the pot-wallopers to safeguard their rights. From then onwards harmonious relations existed between golfers and graziers, and this led to the Northam Urban Council taking over the land and ensuring the continuation of golf. Because the 200 years' tenure of the Manor of Northam was due to expire in 1970, negotiations opened between club and council in 1962. These ended in the council acquiring the remainder of the lease and granting a lease back to the club, conveying the sole right to play golf on the Burrows.

The early history of the Royal North Devon club provides an example of the way in which the public users of common land and those who used it for special purposes could share the amenities in an amicable way. The many commons to be found in or near country villages and in the suburbs of cities are survivals from the medieval system of using the poorest land in the district as a communal space on which the inhabitants had the right to graze their cattle and sheep and to cut wood for fuel. But these rights were enjoyed by the freehold and copyhold tenants of the lord of the manor, whose seigneurial powers were whittled away over the centuries. It was under this system of common rights that the golfers and the pot-wallopers of Westward Ho! shared the use of the Burrows—a satisfactory arrangement for rural communities. But metropolitan commons produced difficult problems owing to the existence of residential areas inhabited by members of the public who, not being freeholders of the lord of manor, were either excluded from open spaces or used them on sufferance. In the middle of the nineteenth century, following the passing of the Enclosure Act of 1845, many acres of common land in Britain were lost to the public, but reformers viewed this development with disquiet, and, largely by their efforts, following attempts by landowners to enclose Wimbledon and Epsom Commons as well as large parts of Epping Forest, the Metropolitan Commons Act was passed in 1866. This effectively stopped further enclosures in the London area, and provided machinery for putting the existing

commons under the control of local authorities or boards of conservators.

During this period of change from the policy of enclosure to one
of public ownership and use, one of the commons in dispute,
Wimbledon, was much favoured by Scottish golfers, and it may
well be that they were among those involved in the dispute arising
from the attempt to enclose this particular open space, on the
south-western outskirts of London. The year following the foundation of Royal North Devon is the birth-date claimed by both the
London Scottish Golf Club and the present Royal Wimbledon Golf
Club. The former was started in 1865 by members of the London
Scottish Rifle Volunteers, and the Wimbledon title was assumed by
seceding members in 1881.

Lord Elcho, MP, afterwards the Earl of Wemyss, was the master
mind of the enterprise, and also the first President, the first captain
being Private R. E. Dudgeon. This juxtaposition of noble lord and
humble private was not so democratic as it might appear to be.
The members of the Corps all sprang from the upper and middle
classes, and Private Dudgeon was a successful doctor. On the golf
course all ranks were equal, and the commanding officer and his
adjutant were members of the committee only *ex officio*.

The choice of Wimbledon as a place for golf arose from the
formation, five years earlier, of the new Volunteer Corps and of the
National Rifle Association. In 1859, after years of negotiation, the
government authorized the formation of Volunteer regiments on a
county basis; a movement which, half a century later, provided a
model for the Territorial Army.

The London Scottish Rifle Volunteers unit was formed in 1859,
the driving force being Lord Elcho, who resigned his seat in
Parliament to become Commanding Officer. At the same time he
and others interested in marksmanship training founded the
National Rifle Association, which now has headquarters at Bisley.
Sidney Herbert, Secretary for War, accepted the Presidency of the
NRA, and a 1,000 yard range was laid out on Wimbledon Common, near the Iron Shooting House used by the London Scottish
volunteers. On 2 July 1860, the range was opened by Queen
Victoria who, under the guidance of Lord Elcho, pulled a string
attached to the trigger of a rifle carefully adjusted for a 400 yard
target. The rifle was fixed on a triangular frame and weighted to
prevent recoil or any other movement; so, not surprisingly, Her
Majesty scored a bull's-eye.

It needs no great flight of imagination to assume that Lord Elcho, heir to a Lothians' earldom and therefore well acquainted with the game played all along that coast which later became known as the golden land of golf, saw the possibilities of Wimbledon Common with its excellent turf and hazards of trees and bushes. It is clear that he and other members played informally over that ground in the years which followed the formation of the Volunteers, and this led to the formation of the London Scottish Golf Club in 1865, a year after the foundation of the Royal North Devon. It may be assumed that all sixteen founder members were Scots, because in the following year the club was 'adopted' into the London Scottish Rifle Volunteers by a Regimental Order dated 2 May 1866. But one of the rules admitted local residents to membership, so very quickly the new club became partly English in character and, of course, partly civilian. This situation held the seeds of discord, for as the years went on the proportion of civilian members grew to outnumber the corps members considerably, and the dual character of the membership created many difficulties which were removed only by a split.

It is impossible to measure now the depth of feeling on both sides in the dispute which raged over the common in 1878 and 1879, but the minutes of the original club show that the exchanges were bitter. The trouble started when the military members, who had a majority in the committee, declined on the score of expense to consider a scheme for moving to better accommodation than that provided in the Iron Shooting House, part of which had been rented from the London Scottish Volunteer Corps in 1871 at an annual rent of £10. Fortunately for the more numerous civilian members, one of them, Mr Henry Lamb, was honorary secretary at that time, and he campaigned unceasingly for a new clubhouse and a better deal for the civilians, who were subjected to the power of veto vested in the commanding officer. The dispute came to a head at the spring general meeting in 1880, when the civilians forced through a resolution limiting the commanding officer's veto to matters directly affecting the corps members. The reaction of the regiment was immediate and dramatic. Colonel Henry Lumsden, who had succeeded Lord Elcho as commanding officer, wrote to Henry Lamb terminating the club's tenancy and suggesting that any member not disposed to acquiesce in regimental control should leave the club 'rather than continue an effort to subvert the basis on which it was founded'.

Most of the civilian members took Colonel Lumsden at his word, and in the following October removed themselves from the Iron House, taking with them their books and trophies and other possessions. They installed themselves in a house not far from the present Royal Wimbledon clubhouse, which they took over two years later. Since the civilian members continued for a while to call themselves the London Scottish Golf Club and the corps members went on playing under the same title, and both clubs have survived to the present day, it seems reasonable to assume that each organization is entitled to claim 1865 as the foundation year. Certainly the honours boards in both clubs list the same captains from 1865 to the year following the split.

Although golf was being played on various open spaces around the capital, Blackheath and London Scottish remained the only clubs in the London area till the foundation of the Clapham Common club in 1873. Some more years elapsed before the formation of the Epsom, Royal Epping Forest and Tooting Bec clubs, all on common land. The Thames Ditton and Esher club on Esher Common and the Prince's club on Mitcham Common followed in 1890, and this did not exhaust the possibilities of golf on England's public spaces. But the patience of golfers was wearing thin as they competed for room not only with unsympathetic members of the public but also with growing numbers of their own kind. The Metropolitan Commons Act gave the public rights for recreational purposes, and the conflicting interests of footballers, cricketers, promenaders, picnickers and golfers created disharmony. The golfers, who were spending money on the maintenance of greens and fairways, were frustrated at every turn, and craved privacy. This need, which the Gentlemen Golfers of Edinburgh had experienced and exploited many years before, was one of the driving forces which brought about the expansion of the 1890s, when golf became a national sport for the English and began its march to world eminence.

CHAPTER 5

From featherie to
guttie ball

Students of nineteenth-century modes and manners would find several reasons for the spread of golf beyond the borders of Scotland, but the most potent of these was the introduction, in mid-century, of a new ball which revolutionized the game. In 1845 the feather ball, or featherie, backed by centuries of use, was seemingly supreme and unchallenged. A few years later it had been superseded completely by a solid ball made from gutta-percha and inevitably called a 'guttie'.

Like so many important inventions, it was the result of a brainwave by which an ordinary and familiar substance was put to a new and exciting use. A St Andrews clergyman, Dr Robert Adam Paterson, having come across some gutta-percha which had been packed round a relic sent from India, probably already knew that it could be softened by heat and would subsequently return to a solid state. This latex, obtained from trees in Malaya, had been in commercial production for many years for making various articles in the Far East, and is said to have been introduced into Britain in the seventeenth century. So for a long time before 1848 someone could have had the idea which seized Dr Paterson as he handled some hard gutta-percha. He cut a small piece, softened it in hot water, and moulded it by hand into a ball. Impressed by the result he took out a patent and apparently negotiated with a London firm for the manufacturing rights. We do know that gutties were in commercial production in 1848, for James Balfour, in his *Reminiscences of Golf on St. Andrews Links* (1887), recalled that his brother-in-law, Admiral Maitland Dougall, played with them in a foursome at Blackheath in that year. The admiral and his partner made the 'interesting discovery' that they flew better at the end of the round than at the beginning.

Mr Balfour wrote 'to London' for a supply and tested the new ball at Musselburgh. John Gourlay, doyen of feather-ball makers, watched the trial and realized his craft was doomed. Having a standing order to send featheries to his patron Sir David Baird whenever he had stock on hand, he despatched six dozen that day; wherefore, recalled Mr Balfour, Sir David was one of the last golfers to adhere to the featherie. Long before that supply was finished, the superiority of the guttie had been generally acknowledged, despite the natural opposition of Gourlay and Robertson and other feather-ball makers. But that dislike was based on groundless fears, and they were shrewd enough to acknowledge eventually that the guttie, of which a dozen could be made in the time spent on one featherie, would transform the game and increase their prosperity. The making of a guttie was an uncomplicated process. A piece of gutta-percha weighing about 1½ ounces was softened in warm water, rolled on a table by hand until it was round, and then allowed to harden. The early gutties were smooth and unpainted, and did not fly well. Wear and tear improved performance—a phenomenon which had been observed at Blackheath by Admiral Dougall and his partner—and it was not long before someone hit on the idea of reproducing artificially the cuts and bruises which gave the guttie its aerodynamic qualities. The newly-made ball was nicked all over by the sharp end of a hammer, and from that device to the production of moulds having patterns on their inner surfaces was but a step. The moulds could produce ball after ball of identical weight, size and pattern, and for the first time in its long history golf had a missile which ensured consistency of performance.

The guttie was chiefly responsible for the rapid spread of golf outside Scotland during the latter half of the nineteenth century. There were other factors, of course. The Industrial Revolution had brought a great accession of national wealth. The railways were spreading through the land to provide cheap and rapid transport. The urge for reform had put enterprising ideas into receptive heads; and sport, which now plays so large a part in the average Englishman's life, was just beginning to capture the public imagination. In such conditions a new game was bound to attract interest, but it had to be easy to understand and play, and not too expensive. These requirements were provided by the guttie ball— more reliable in behaviour than the featherie, more durable, and infinitely cheaper. It is probable that many visitors to Scotland for holidays in the eighteenth and early nineteenth centuries would have been attracted to the game if a ball like the guttie, easily and cheaply produced, had been in use.

Although the playing characteristics of the new ball gave it consistency, it flew no farther than had the featherie when struck by an expert. Its chief advantage was greater accuracy, both in flight and on the putting green. The improvement in putting quality was important because courses now had fair-sized greens in as good a condition as the unsophisticated green-keeping of the times could achieve. Until well into the nineteenth century the 'greens' were small scythed patches around the hole. The early 1744 rules stated that the ball had to be teed for driving within a club's length of the hole just used, and since the player usually took sand from that hole to build a tee, and often scraped the turf in driving, anything like a putt as it is understood today would have been impossible. The emphasis was on approach play, with the aim of getting the lofted shot so near to the hole that the ball could be coaxed in with the long-headed wooden putter. In 1777 the teeing-ground was described as 'not nearer than one club-length nor further than four club-lengths from the hole'. In 1828 the minimum distance was increased to two club-lengths, and by mid-century this had become six club-lengths, providing a green of about seven yards radius from the flagstick. When the guttie age began, therefore, the average green had become a recognizable well-mown surface used only for putting, and therefore demonstrated the imperfections of the featherie, because a true roll had become essential.

Any comparison between the distances achieved by featherie and guttie is impossible in the absence of any reliable statistics. Samuel Messieux, a French schoolmaster, and twice winner of the R. and A. scratch Gold Medal in 1825 and 1828, has been credited with a drive of 361 yards with a featherie, but this must have been an exceptional performance in freak conditions, and the absence of authentic statistics may be due to the fact that in those days distance was not so important as it is now. Keeping the ball in play and avoiding trouble were the golfer's main preoccupations. Statistics for the guttie are more plentiful. In 1892 Edward Blackwell, a very powerful man, drove a guttie, helped by a following wind, from the 18th tee at St Andrews to the steps of the R. and A. clubhouse, a distance of 366 yards. But around the same time, tests carried out by Douglas Rolland, the longest driver among the professionals, produced an average of 205 yards, his longest hit being 235 yards.

It is possible that the best featherie was longer in flight than the best guttie. But its disadvantages—malformation, inconsistency, costliness and short life—doomed it to extinction once a better substitute had been found. The guttie, easily made, low in cost, hard-wearing and repairable, had to be struck well to give of its best, but that was relatively unimportant. It provided a considerable advance and wrought the first great change in golf, which quickly developed in popularity and scope. The advent of the guttie brought about a revolution which, like all revolutions, produced new men, new ideas, new standards.

CHAPTER 6

The pioneer professionals

One important effect of the spread of golf was the emergence of the professional as member of a distinct class. It is doubtful if that description was applied to anyone before the middle of the nineteenth century, and in 1860 only eight professionals were invited to compete in the first Open Championship. Alan Robertson, born at St Andrews in 1815, and trained to be a maker of feather balls in the footsteps of his father and grandfather, is generally regarded as the first of the true professionals. Before his day history has recorded only men who, as caddies, club-makers, ball-makers or greenkeepers, made golf their livelihood. Early in 1603 William Mayne, an Edinburgh bowmaker, was appointed club-maker to James VI of Scotland, who, fifteen years later, as James I of the United Kingdom, granted the ball monopoly to James Melville, already mentioned.

Nothing is known of Mayne's skill as a club-maker, and the craft was probably in its infancy. The next club-maker to be noticed was Andrew Dickson, who also acted as caddie to the Duke of York when the future James II played golf at Leith in 1681–2, during his residence in Edinburgh as commissioner from Charles II to the Scottish Parliament. Caddies were then employed not only as carriers of clubs, which they held loose in the crook of the arm, but also for finding balls driven into trouble on links which abounded in bushes, gorse, sandy hazards, ditches and broken ground. The caddie, having handed the required club to the player, would run forwards to mark the fall of the ball. He would also give advice on choice of club or the line of a putt and was usually competent to give instruction to a beginner. Dickson was more than a mere club-carrier, for he also made clubs and knew how to use them, but there is no evidence that he or his contemporaries had high rank as players. Indeed there is evidence to the contrary, for when the Duke sought a suitable partner who could help him win an important match, he was recommended not to a caddie or a club-maker, but to a shoemaker who was the seventeenth-century equivalent of the present-day artisan amateur.

John Patersone was reputed to be among the best golfers who then played on Leith links, and golf, not cobbling, made his fortune. The Duke had accepted a challenge from two English noblemen to a foursome match, he to have any Scottish partner he chose. Seeking popularity with the citizens and anxious to ensure success, he chose the shoemaker in preference to one of his retinue. The match ended in an easy victory for the Duke and the cobbler, and the future James II, delighted with the outcome, gave Patersone half the stake won. With that money Patersone built a house in the Canongate, with a coat of arms fixed to the wall showing a dexter hand grasping a golf club, with the motto 'Far and Sure'.

Had he lived in these times, the cobbler would have found it difficult to substantiate a claim to be an amateur. But in the seventeenth century such a distinction was unknown, and for two centuries afterwards no rule existed to distinguish amateurs from professionals. The current rule book devotes something like two thousand words to the matter, but when the first golf clubs were formed many an artisan who was good at the game could make money by his skill without comment. And the gentleman golfer could wager heavily on the fortunes of his side without blemish on his standing as one who played the game purely for fun. By the time Allan Robertson reached manhood the increase in the number of players and courses created a demand for the services which professionals could give, and the best players found patrons among the local gentlemen. They were employed in several ways, including club-carrying and instruction, but also, and to an increasing extent, in matches for side-stakes against each other or with amateur partners in foursomes. Robertson was a pawky Scot with business instincts who was able to employ workmen to make clubs and balls, and so could give his main attention to playing, sometimes backed by amateurs but often carrying his own colours. By his skill he earned recognition as the first of the great players, and had he recovered fully from an attack of jaundice which ended his life in 1859 the early history of the Open Championship, which started in the following year, might well have included his name alongside those of his one-time partner Old Tom Morris and Musselburgh's pride Willie Park, who between them won the title eight times. Only a few months before his illness Robertson went round the Old Course at St Andrews in 79, at a time when the best amateurs there, including many who would have been rated scratch if a handicapping system had existed, were rarely beating 100 in the R. and A. Medal competitions.

Robertson, reputed never to have lost a singles match on level terms, was much more than a talented player. He was a hard worker for the good of St Andrews golf, and one of the most loved and respected figures. When he was a boy, all those who worked for golf were considered as one class, and there was little to distinguish the caddie from the master ballmaker. Long before he died, this large class had split into sub-classes, and one of the most important was that composed of craftsmen who flourished in the first half of the nineteenth century. Two of the best known were contemporaries and each a master in his field—John Gourlay and Hugh Philp. Gourlay, a Musselburgh man who died in 1869, was the most celebrated ball-maker in the fruitful years of that trade. He was official ball-maker to the Edinburgh Burgess Society, and survived to see the guttie ball destroy the craft at which he had excelled for many years. Philp, a maker of golf clubs and particularly renowned for his wooden putters with their long pear-shaped heads, was born at St Andrews in 1772 and worked as a carpenter who, from repairing clubs, took to making them. In 1827 he was appointed club-maker to the Society of St Andrews golfers, as a tribute to his outstanding skill.

Allan Robertson had the most influential position at St Andrews, but although he placed himself at the disposal of the R. and A. members and was virtually professional to the club, the title was never conferred on him because the job did not exist. Tom Morris was not then in the position he was to occupy much later, and when the newly-formed Prestwick club offered him a job as professional at 15s. a week, in 1853, he went to the Ayrshire coast. To be a professional attached to a club was new enough in those days to make the Prestwick move a step up the ladder for Morris, and although his duties included superintendence of the green-keeping work, he no doubt saw the chance of augmenting his basic wage by playing and teaching. Meanwhile, back at St Andrews, the R. and A. members were becoming interested in the idea of having someone under their control to minister to their needs and look after the course. For some years the Old Course had been tended by David

(Old Daw) Anderson, whose son Jamie won the Open three years running. Old Daw was once a ball-maker employed by Robertson. He was also at times a caddie, and after his retirement from course maintenance duties he kept a ginger-beer stall on the links. It was during his time that separate holes were cut for outward and inward play. Before 1851 the holes used by players going out to the ninth were putted into by those on the homeward journey, an arrangement necessitated by the narrowness of the links between masses of gorse. On busy days there was much frustration for golfers forced to wait before approaching greens on which others, playing in the opposite direction, were putting. The widening of the course by removing much of the gorse and cutting separate 'homeward' holes brought about the construction of the huge double greens, seven serving fourteen holes, which are features of the Old Course to this day.

On the retirement of David Anderson the club appointed Walter Alexander and Alexander Herd to look after the course. They were not expert green-keepers, merely promoted caddies, and no doubt, for the £6 a year they shared, put more brawn than brain into the job. They were certainly not professionals, but in 1863 the R. and A. decided to appoint someone to serve the club in that capacity and also to take charge of the course work. Robertson was dead and the obvious candidate was Morris, who for two years running had won the Open Championship at Prestwick, beating his great rival Willie Park each time. So Morris came home from Prestwick and began a long and distinguished connection with the home of golf which ended only with his death forty-five years later. In bare financial terms the move back to St Andrews was scarcely an improvement on Prestwick. He was engaged at £50 per year and his duties were defined as keeping the putting greens in good order, repairing worn places, and general maintenance. He was allowed one man's labour for two days a week and £20 a year for the cost of materials and tools. Nevertheless he was back at St Andrews, the acknowledged successor to Robertson, and we may be sure that his duties on the course were allowed neither by him nor his employers to affect his playing activities.

Although Willie Park did not hold a club appointment at Musselburgh—to this day the Honourable Company do not employ a professional—he was a successful freelance as a purveyor of clubs and balls to Musselburgh golfers, and a player who never hesitated to back himself in matches. But there were few professionals, whether attached or unattached, in mid-century. It is true that the first Open Championship was by invitation, but in 1861, when it was thrown open to the world, only ten professionals came forward, and another thirty years passed before the total reached forty. Nevertheless, those thirty years saw many changes, particularly in the character, behaviour and status of the professional. The competitors in the first Open were rough-and-ready sons of the links, dressed in baggy reach-me-downs and coarse woollen coats, and with a variety of headgear from tarpaulin caps to bonnets. Their clubs were carried by caddies who were removed very little, if at all, from their employers in the social scale, and therefore indulged in familiarity which would not be tolerated today.

Professional golfers of those days were a bohemian lot and most of them were accustomed to gather in a bar after play and exchange conversation and drinks with everyone, including their caddies. Serious church-going Tom Morris and business-like Willie Park no doubt maintained some exclusiveness, but they must have found it difficult to avoid the familiarity of their fellows. The life of those men was neither affluent nor secure. The best players today are so glamorized by the public and reap such rich rewards, on and off the course, that it is difficult to imagine a period when the professional was regarded as among the lower forms of human life on the links. His occupation was not considered respectable, and those who followed it were often of humble birth, poor in circumstances and lacking good education. Many worked at regular trades, partly because it was impossible to rely on golf alone for subsistence, partly because it was essential to have a craft to fall back on in the event of bad times. There were few opportunities for competition and the prizes were small. Organized teaching was unknown and amateur patrons gave rewards depending on individual inclinations rather than on fixed scales. A few, like Robertson, Morris and Park and several who followed them, enjoyed reasonable incomes from making and selling clubs and balls, and were much in demand as playing partners for amateurs and contestants in challenge matches. But they were the fortunate exceptions and most of their fellows led a haphazard existence.

Those who followed trades had usually been persuaded by their parents to apprentice themselves to worthwhile occupations, because golf, in the opinion of the elders, was considered a precarious calling which encouraged fecklessness, indiscipline and low living. More than one Open Champion spent his early life in this way. Willie Fernie, who won the title in 1883, Jack Burns, the 1888 champion, and Sandy Herd, who in 1902 was the first winner to use the newly-introduced rubber-core ball, all served their time as apprentices to Andrew Scott, a master plasterer and prominent member of the St Andrews Golf Club, an organization of artisans and tradesmen to which several professionals belonged. Andrew Kirkaldy, who twice nearly won the Open and later was professional to the Royal and Ancient club, spent many of his best years as a soldier in the Black Watch, and Willie Park's brother Mungo was a sailor before he took up golf seriously and became champion in 1874.

Fernie worked as a journeyman-plasterer between golfing engagements, and travelled to tournaments and matches in the donkey-cart he used for his work, often taking fellow-professionals as passengers. These men undertook journeys of fifty miles or more to play for modest prizes, and the majority would return empty-handed. Andrew Kirkaldy, recollecting a trip with Fernie to a competition at Wemyss, about twenty miles from St Andrews, in which he won the fourth prize of thirty shillings, once observed (in Kirkaldy's *Fifty Years of Golf: My Memories*, 1921, see pages 15–16):

> Professional golfers were not pampered when I was young. We were kept in our place and never allowed to get purse-proud. But the winners didn't forget the losers. There was a good deal of playing for the glory and sharing the spoils, or spending it in the good old-fashioned style.

An adjournment to the nearest inn after play meant that the losers shared in the entertainment by the generosity of the winners, and the innkeeper retained most of the prize-money.

The early life of Sandy Herd was typical of the evolution of a champion in Victorian days. He was born at St Andrews in 1868 and played his first golf strokes in the streets in company with other boys, using whatever came to hand as substitutes for balls. Corks with nails driven through them to give stability were favourite missiles, but whatever they had was used with enthusiasm. Sandy soon showed great promise and wanted to earn his living at golf, but met with strong parental opposition. 'A life for a ne'er-do-well', was his mother's condemnation, and, to provide him with a 'respectable' trade, he was apprenticed to a baker at the age of eleven. After four years in the bakehouse he apprenticed himself to Andrew

Scott, probably influenced by the fact that one of his predecessors in the plasterer's shed, Willie Fernie, had just won the Open Championship. The work was hard and the hours long but no son of St Andrews with golf in his heart could be deterred by anything from playing whenever he could, and Sandy made the best use of his spare time. In 1886, three years after starting his new trade, he joined St Andrews Golf Club and a few months later, aged only eighteen, won the club's Scratch Medal.

In 1892 he set off for Muirfield to compete in the Open for the first time. He played in the rough jacket and white fustian trousers he wore at work, and his modest set of four clubs—driver, spoon, mid-iron and a cleek doubling as putter—was carried under-arm by a younger brother. The recollection of that début must often have come into Sandy's mind when, years later, he was professional at Moor Park, with a shop in one wing of the stately mansion which served as clubhouse.

The uncertainties of professional golf in the nineteenth century can be judged from the career of Jack Burns. He broke away from the plastering trade after serving his time and went on the railway as a platelayer. In 1886 he took a job as professional-greenkeeper at the newly-opened Warwickshire Golf Club. Two years later he won the Open at St Andrews, but this brought him so little reward or renown that he soon gave up professional golf and returned to the railway. Fortunately for posterity most of Burns's contemporaries were more tenacious. Herd in particular never lost his keenness and his confidence in the future of golf. There is a story about him and George Hirst, the famous Yorkshire cricketer, at a time when Herd was professional at the Huddersfield club and therefore in constant contact with those who regarded cricket as the greatest game. When Sandy declared that golf would one day be the national game, Hirst demurred. 'In Scotland, maybe, because Scotland is too hilly and the climate too chilly for cricket.' 'I shouldn't wonder,' replied Sandy, 'if we both lived to see the day when golf will be the universal game, because it suits all climates.' They did.

CHAPTER 7

Amateurism—the great split

Social development, it has been said, increases the complexities of existence and creates fresh dangers for the community. The argument, intended to refer to society in a general sense, can be applied to golf with the qualification that the disadvantages of the changes which occurred in the middle of the nineteenth century were more than offset by subsequent benefits. Before that time the simplicity of the game and the restricted area in which it was played preserved it from complications but limited its scope. The expansion stemming from the introduction of the gutta-percha ball and the spread of golf throughout England inevitably created problems which the Scottish pioneers had never encountered. Just as enrichment of the soil produces not only good plants but also vigorous weeds which must be removed before they become troublesome, so Victorian golf, deriving nourishment from the national progress towards unprecedented prosperity for the middle classes, was beset by difficulties which only time and wise government could eliminate, or at least control.

One of the more obvious illustrations of the growing complexity of golf legislation was the initial difficulty of distinguishing between amateurs and professionals. When the Gentlemen of Edinburgh and St Andrews were establishing themselves with competitions and private quarters, no line of demarcation had to be drawn because it was plain enough in the abstract, maintained by the gentlemen amateurs as a natural right and observed by others with equally natural respect. The only rule was one of social standing. One did or did not 'belong' and those who did not were collectively outside the pale, whether they were clubmakers, caddies, tradesmen or artisans. There was no need for finer distinctions. Those outside the select circle played golf when and how they could and were able to win prize-money without being criticized or penalized. Gentlemen played for money, too, in the form of side-stakes—often for big money; but so far from being accused of commercializing their skill, they were respected as sportsmen willing to back their performances. It was an age when gambling was an essential part of social life.

Until the start of the Open Championship it was unknown for a gentleman amateur to play in a competition alongside a tradesman or an artisan. Both classes were often represented in matches, as opponents or partners, but never appeared together in contests for the same prizes. In time, golfers outside the gentleman class formed their own clubs and fraternities and ran competitions which were in their way just as exclusive as those for the silver clubs. The first Open Championship was contested only by professionals invited to take part, but in 1861 it was declared open and amateurs were able to enter. This was an entirely new departure and destined to be one of the factors in creating an official definition of professionalism. In 1890 John Ball of Hoylake scored the first amateur victory in that event, and by that time rules governing amateur status existed. But if an amateur had won in the earlier years, he would probably have accepted quite naturally the money prize as well as the title, and would not have been stigmatized for so doing. He and his fellows would have viewed the matter as casually as the present-day golfer regards the winning of a sweepstake. The career of John Ball himself provides evidence on this point. He competed in the Open for the first time in 1876, aged fifteen, finished sixth and received 10*s.*, the allotted prize for that place. There was no criticism, official or otherwise, of John Ball's action and this was due not to the insignificant sum involved, but to the absence of any need to use the acceptance of prize-money as a factor in distinguishing between the classes.

The free-and-easy conditions in the middle of the nineteenth century are illustrated by the early history of the St Andrews Golf Club, formed in 1843 by a number of citizens who would not have been considered for membership of the R. and A., nor would have wished to apply. They enjoyed the privilege of free play over ground which belonged to them, as their ancestors had done from earliest times, and had no need to organize for the purpose of protecting their rights. The desire for a corporate existence to pursue friendly activities animated them, as it had animated the founders of the R. and A., but the character of the new club was clearly indicated by its original title—the St Andrews Mechanics' Golf Club—and in the status of its eleven founder members. They were three cabinet-makers, a stonemason, a joiner, a tailor, a plasterer, a slater, a house-painter, a butler and a dancing-master. The last-named, James McPherson, supplemented his income by selling and repairing golf clubs. The butler was Tom Morris's brother George, who seems to have retained his non-professional status throughout, leaving Tom and his two sons, Young Tommy and 'Jof', to become leading professionals. Old Tom was a member of the club in its early years. So was Allan Robertson, who served as captain in 1853. There is no evidence that either played in the club's competitions, but several others did who were professionals at the time or later. Apart from the Morrises the St Andrews members included eleven who subsequently won the Open Championship.

For a long time there was no suggestion that the club was wrong to admit professionals as members, and when Willie Fernie won the Open in 1883 he was the seventh member to hold the title. But events were moving towards the establishment of a distinction between amateurs and professionals. In 1885 the Open was played on the Old Course, and all the best golfers in the St Andrews club entered. They included Jack Burns the plasterer, who did well enough in the championship (won by Bob Martin, a former member) to receive one of the cash prizes. Later that year Burns competed for the club's autumn medal, which he had won previously in 1883, and returned the best score, 88. William Greig, who had also played in the Championship, finished second with 89, but at a special meeting it was proposed to pass over Burns and Greig and award the medal to R. Braid, who had returned the third best score, 91. There was a terrific row, but the decision was left to the committee, which decided that Jack Burns be disqualified because he had taken money in the championship, and that he be barred from playing otherwise than as an honorary member of the club. This meant that he could play in inter-club matches but not in competitions. Greig was awarded the medal in accordance with an understanding that members of the club could enter the championship and hold the cup, if successful, but not receive prize-money. A special general meeting had to be convened before the committee's ruling was upheld, and so a protracted dispute ended in the first positive step towards regularizing an irregular situation. By implication, a definition of a professional had been reached—one who accepts prize-money.

The outcome of this fracas may not have excited anyone but those immediately concerned—it was probably regarded as a domestic matter—but later that year a similar ruling by another club brought home to the whole world of golf the need for legislation about amateurism. The leading clubs held regular medal competitions, usually in spring and autumn, and as many amateurs were members of more than one, it was customary to stagger the dates to allow those eligible to compete for each medal in turn. These congregations of the best amateur players and the prowess of their own star member, John Ball, inspired the members of the Liverpool club to promote an open amateur knock-out tournament at Hoylake. This was so successful that it led to the institution in the following year, 1886, of the Amateur Championship. Many years later, in 1919, the Hoylake event was officially designated the first Amateur Championship and the name of Alan F. MacFie recorded in the list of winners.

Naturally every amateur of note in the country entered for the 1885 competition and they included Douglas Rolland, a stonemason from Elie in Fife, who was already famed as a long driver, and had recently beaten John Ball in a challenge match. In the previous year the Open Championship had been won by Jack Simpson, another stonemason from Carnoustie; and Rolland, being joint runner-up with Willie Fernie, shared with him the prize-money for second and third places. This fact was recalled when Rolland entered for the Hoylake competition, and after much debate the organizing committee rejected his entry. It was decided that, by accepting prize-money, he had offended against a rule, common to all sports, that an amateur could not receive a money prize when competing with professionals.

In this case, as with the St Andrews Golf Club, a private club had reached a decision on a domestic matter, and had not invoked the rules of golf because there was no rule regarding amateurism and the rules themselves not yet binding on everyone. But the Hoylake decision, following that of the St Andrews club, was of vital importance and had an immediate sequel. Those responsible for promoting the first official Amateur Championship in 1886 had to consider the best means of deciding eligibility. Until then, with club competitions the only amateur fixtures, a definition had been unnecessary. Private clubs admitted only those who were socially acceptable and naturally their doors were closed to artisans and professionals alike. The Douglas Rolland case made the private clubs, who controlled the championships, painfully aware of the need for ensuring that only amateurs played in amateur events. So they ruled that, for the purpose of competing in the new championship, an amateur golfer

> shall be a golfer who has never made for sale any golf clubs, balls, or any other articles connected with the game, who has never carried clubs for hire after attaining the age of 15 years, and who has not carried clubs for hire at any time within 6 years of the date on which the competition begins in each year; who has never received any consideration for playing in a match or for giving lessons in the game, and who, for a period of five years prior to the 1st. of September, 1886, has never received a money prize in an open competition.

Discussions on this construction had been influenced by rules adopted in other sports. In 1865 the English Amateur Athletic Club had defined an amateur as

> Any gentleman who has never competed in an open competition nor for public payment nor admission money, nor with a professional for a prize, public money, or admission money: who has never at any period of his life taught, pursued, or assisted in the pursuit of athletic exercises as a means of livelihood, and is not a tradesman, mechanic, artisan or labourer.

Two definitions with a significant difference. That adopted for golf was confined to the question of gaining materially from playing or serving, but the rule for athletes closed the door to everyone below a certain class. The exclusion of tradesmen, mechanics, artisans and labourers was abandoned not long afterwards in athletics, but retained until after the Great War by the Amateur Rowing Association, which controlled Henley Regatta and other important events. The National Amateur Rowing Association catered for the many clubs which could not be considered 'amateur' under the ARA definition, and eventually the ARA had to climb down from their original attitude. But there is still much hypocrisy in this matter, and nothing since 1958 has happened to change the views I expressed then in my book *Golfers at Law* (pages 134–5):

> Who is and who is not an amateur sportsman? The literal meaning—a lover of the game for the game's sake—has lost much of its original significance owing to . . . the taint of commercialism A century ago there was no need for rules about amateurism An amateur played for fun at his own expense and a

professional was paid for playing The amateur sometimes won money by wagering on his skill; the professional sometimes had to play only for fun; but that did not alter the distinction between them Then commercialism crept in. Golf became an industry. The newspapers took interest and then came the publicity of radio and television. It is difficult to distinguish between the representative of a golf ball firm who wins a championship and the championship winner who gets a job with a golf firm; between the golf writer who becomes an international and the international who takes to writing about golf. Who is to say whether the promising young amateur who gets a post in the office of a golf-keen stockbroker is preferred for his promise at golf or his potential as a financier?

In recent years there have been cases, in cricket and lawn tennis for example, where the golden rule of amateurism has been corrupted out of existence by circumstances dictated by commercialism and the sheer impossibility of preserving a race of sportsmen of independent means and unlimited time, in sufficient numbers to maintain a distinction between pure amateurs and pseudo-professionals. At one time I envisaged the possibility of merging the two classes in golf, as has happened with some other sports. But the golf legislators on both sides of the Atlantic have striven and are striving to preserve amateurism, although they have had to adjust their original hard line to suit changing circumstances.

During 1970 and 1971 the R. and A. investigated the feasibility of defining a 'professional' and treating all others as amateurs; but the idea was abandoned mainly because it would not remove the existing borderline cases which had created the demand for a more liberal interpretation of the rules. On the other hand the Rules of Golf Committee realized the danger of creating, by too much liberalization, an amateur élite or 'third category'. It was a question of compromise, and on 1 January 1974, the R. and A., with the general agreement of affiliated and associated bodies, introduced revised amateur laws which did at least remove one considerable cause of complaint—that the rules favoured young golfers in comfortable financial circumstances and handicapped those less well off.

This class distinction by rule had existed for nearly a hundred years. It was created by the first rules of amateurism in 1886 and ever since had prevented the impecunious youngster from obtaining any financial help towards the cost of playing, except through his father or legal guardian. The 1974 revision dealt with that in two ways. A player of any age can now be financed by a legal guardian or a member of his family—a wide definition which covers uncles, aunts, cousins, brothers, sisters, and grandparents. The other important alteration allowed a National or County Union to pay the expenses of any golfer under twenty-two to play as an individual in a national or county event. The old rule allowed this to be done only for members of representative teams and in connection with the team event in which they played. It is also now permissible for commercial sponsors to encourage promising youngsters provided that any money involved is paid only to the National or County Union concerned to be used at the discretion of that body.

These decisions were in line with current discontent with the existing rules as having a restrictive effect on the progress of many young players, and also counteracted to some extent the considerable advantage so far enjoyed by the United States with their scholarships system. In the alterations, St Andrews made a big step towards the modern concept of free opportunities for everyone, irrespective of class. This had been recognized from the start of American golf, as might be expected in such a democratic atmosphere, with the result that young Americans, with the help of caddie and other scholarships, college golf squads and inter-college contests, have always had far greater scope for developing their talents within the amateur laws.

It would seem that the liberalization process in Britain could be taken a stage further by introducing some version of the US scholarship schemes. But the problem of preserving amateurism has been helped by the development of big prize-money tournaments and worthwhile fringe benefits, making the rewards of professionalism high enough to justify a player making a clean break from his former status. The modern amateur often has his thoughts set on winning international honours and titles in that field with the intention, if successful, of turning professional. This attitude, which would have horrified golfers of two generations ago, is typical of the times, yet has an affinity with the thinking of 1886 when it was first found necessary to define distinctions previously accepted without debate.

CHAPTER 8

Search for privacy on the links

One inevitable result of the spread of golf away from the traditional centres of the east coast of Scotland was a tendency for men to seek exclusiveness for their own particular circles. Until the middle of the eighteenth century, golfers had mingled freely on the common links regardless of social distinctions, and even when the upper classes formed societies they still had to compete on equal terms with everyone else for the use of playing facilities. Those early clubs or societies were exclusive and private only in their control of membership and their activities off the course. After playing they went to their clubrooms, in those days merely private rooms in inns. As they often shouldered at their own expense the responsibility for keeping the links in good order and introducing improvements, they naturally sought seclusion also in play. But the only privileges obtainable on the public links were those conceded by inferiors to superiors and inspired by natural respect and material considerations. For these reasons the gentlemen golfers gradually acquired a separate status, but as the golf population grew so did their sense of frustration. That is why the Burgess golfers of Bruntsfield and the Honourable Gentlemen of Leith both went to Musselburgh, and finally to private grounds at Barnton and Muirfield respectively.

Their example was followed by many other clubs in Scotland, but when golf was adopted by the English in the nineteenth century the development proceeded as it had done in Scotland originally. Members of the Old Manchester club played on the open moor. Blackheath pioneers used rough common land shared with non-playing citizens. So did the early Wimbledon golfers and those who played at Clapham, Mitcham and other places. Such places, like the Scottish links, were sufficiently open for the purpose, free of charge, and required a minimum expenditure of time and money on maintenance. But there was an important social difference. In Scotland everyone played, whereas in England the game was restricted at first to men of leisure and means, the lower classes coming into contact with it only as servants. In Scotland those who did use the links for other purposes were nearly all golfers and therefore respected the activities of those who played. But many of the citizens who walked on the English commons were either indifferent or openly hostile, their reactions ranging from obstinate refusal to give way, to acts of aggressive vandalism. Similar animosity on the part of the pot-wallopers of Westward Ho! had been tempered in time by financial and social pressures, but those living and working in the big cities had a more independent outlook and were disinclined to concede priority to anyone, least of all those following upper-class pastimes. They had no concern at all for the protection of those parts of the ground used for golf, and putting greens for them were merely excellent places for playing cricket or enjoying picnics. So far from respecting the efforts of golfers to preserve the golfing ground, they regarded this as infringement of their public rights.

The old Blackheath course provided an excellent example of the trials of playing golf on common land. There were only seven holes and the greens were difficult to distinguish since they scarcely differed from the rest of the heath, worn as it was by the feet of pedestrians. The hazards were disused gravel pits, a pond, and various roads and paths. The teeing-grounds, such as they were, were marked on competition days by a dab of whitewash. There were no teeboxes or other markers, no flags on the greens, and the player approaching a green sent his caddie forward to stand by the hole. Sand for the tees was carried in the caddies' pockets. From very early days golf on Blackheath had been free, but early in the present century the London County Council not only imposed a charge but insisted that players must wear red coats and be preceded by a forecaddie carrying a red flag. By this time conditions had become so chaotic that golf on Blackheath was more painful than pleasant. Then came the Great War in 1914. The heath was taken over for mules, guns and searchlights, and that was the end of England's oldest golf links.

It says much for the endurance of those old Blackheath golfers that they went on playing there in spite of the gravel pits, the roads, the picnic parties, the lamp-posts and the nursemaids' prams. Adherence to tradition was a powerful influence, as well as the accessibility of the place for those tied for various reasons to the capital. But many of the Blackheath golfers were also members of clubs further out from London and in more pleasant and private surroundings, and so had the opportunity to 'get away from it all' at week-ends.

At Wimbledon the conditions were almost idyllic by comparison. The locals were more respectful towards their betters, the ground was more extensive, allowing for the laying out of a full course; and although the rules of the common allowed play on only three days a week, with red coats obligatory at all times, the advantages far outweighed the disadvantages. But the Wimbledon golfers still experienced the annoyance of having a golf course maintained by them invaded at times by members of the public, and this frustration was suffered by other early golfers in many parts of the country. Those of Westward Ho! were luckier, for North Devon was not out of the way for men of independent means and unlimited leisure, who often went there from Scotland, northern England and the London area for long week-ends or summer holidays. It was a different matter for those with business or professional ties who required playing facilities within easy reach of office and home, and accessibility and suitability were rarely found in the same place. The tradition that golf was a seaside game was still strong, and pioneers in Cheshire and Lancashire were fortunate to find stretches of wonderful golfing country along their coastline. Liverpool was the springboard for a number of projects during the last thirty years of the nineteenth century, beginning in 1869 with the formation of the Liverpool (later Royal) club on the shores of the Dee estuary, near the little fishing village of Hoylake. The village is now a town, almost part of the conurbation of Liverpool and Birkenhead, but in those days was remote enough to be safe from invasion by non-golfers, except on the few days each year when the modest racecourse was in use for meetings.

The early holes at Hoylake were made inside the racecourse, and the club's first quarters were in the Royal Hotel, owned by John Ball's father, which is now separated by a road from the present 17th green. That point was the start of the original round as it was in 1885 for the event which subsequently became the Amateur Championship. In 1897 the Open Championship was played at Hoylake for the first time, and in preparation the Liverpool golfers re-planned the course and built the present clubhouse on the other side. Long before this, other golfers had exploited the coastline to the north of Liverpool. In 1873 the West Lancs club was established among the sandhills at Blundellsands, and from there development spread northwards to embrace such famous links as Formby, Southport and Ainsdale, Hillside, Birkdale, and Lytham St Annes. The Formby club at Freshfield began in 1884, the course being ideally suited, within walking distance of a station yet in the middle of a pine forest next to the sea. In 1885 the Southport (later Hesketh) club was founded and a year later the Lytham links, now the home of the Royal Lytham and St Annes club. The Birkdale club, now Royal Birkdale and the most important centre for big golf in England, came in 1889. There were also interesting developments in other parts of England. At the foot of the Malvern Hills, golfers from Birmingham and district founded the Worcestershire club in 1879, on common land, and in 1882 the formation of the Great Yarmouth club saw the start of golf in East Anglia. Soon afterwards Dr Laidlaw Purves and Mr Henry Lamb, members of the Wimbledon Club, were travelling by train from Canterbury to Dover when they saw a range of sandhills stretching from Pegwell Bay to the outskirts of Deal. A glimpse was enough. They investigated, planned and organized, and in 1887 the Royal St George's links came into existence—far from the risk of intrusion by the public, as private and as snug as anyone could wish. No cattle, no pot-wallopers, no picnic parties. Only the perfect seaside turf, the natural sand bunkers, the sea and the sky, and in the sky the trilling larks.

Something new had happened for golfers with time and money to spare. The train from Charing Cross could transport them in two or three hours from the grime of London to the pure Kentish seaside air, and give them week-end golf. Very soon the Kent coast became a playground for golfers. The Littlestone club started at New Romney in 1888, and four years later came the Royal Cinque Ports links at Deal. Another ideal spot was found north of Yarmouth at Brancaster, home of the Royal West Norfolk club, and by the end of the 1880s there were many places in England, mainly on the coast, where the growing band of English golfers could play under pleasant and uninhibited conditions. Nevertheless most of these desirable places were remote from the main centres of population, and as the golfers increased in number so did their need for grounds on which they could play in privacy and comfort without having to make long journeys. Those living in Liverpool and Preston were fortunate in having so much fine golfing country close at hand. But those in big cities inland were less comfortably placed because the few available open spaces were gradually being surrounded, sometimes even eroded, by building developments. The problem had to be solved if golf was to become a pastime for millions and not remain the recreation of a privileged few.

The last Victorian decade was a time of significant social changes and golf was not least susceptible to the effects of the shift from strait-laced conformity and snobbish class-consciousness to comparatively free-and-easy attitudes of mind and behaviour. Britons generally still valued moral and religious virtues and recognized social distinctions, but gay society led by the Prince of Wales was following a new code of conduct, and the middle classes were rising in prestige and importance. Such changes inevitably affected golf in England. It had always been a democratic game in Scotland, where everyone could play freely on the common links and only such factors as leisure time, more money and respect from subordinates gave the upper classes priority. English golf lacked those traditions and the earliest English pioneers were nearly all from the well-to-do and well-born members of a recognized social order. But as the game spread there was an ever-increasing demand, by an ever-widening middle section of the population, for sophisticated playing facilities.

This represented a marked change from the situation at the time of the formation of the North Devon and London Scottish clubs. Then no one outside a small circle had any knowledge of the game or any incentive or inclination to gain knowledge. The middle classes in their respectable domestic lives were not brought into direct contact with it, and the working classes saw it as an object of ridicule and contempt except where, in certain localities, it was a source of casual employment. Those knickerbockered men who played at Sandwich, Westward Ho! and Hoylake and other places away from the cities were deemed a little odd, if not completely crazy, by ordinary citizens who observed them in transit. A bag of clubs and its owner on any railway station platform, except those serving golf centres, often aroused curiosity and became the target for polite amused stares, light jesting or ribald comment. (Such attitudes were prevalent even as late as 1906, as the *Punch* cartoon, reproduced here as Plate 4, shows.) For many years golf had been played on Blackheath, certainly since the eighteenth century if not continuously since Stuart times, so there was at least one locality in Victorian London where the inhabitants were accustomed to watching the antics of players. We can only guess at the thoughts of Blackheath residents as they saw elderly gentlemen, obviously respectable and apparently in full possession of their senses, pursuing a small ball over the broken ground and becoming hot and bothered in the process.

As the start of organized golf on Wimbledon Common was followed by similar experiments elsewhere, on the commons of Clapham, Tooting, Mitcham, non-golfing inhabitants of London and other big cities were aware that some people played golf. The humbler citizens tended to regard it as outside their comprehension. They described as 'ockey-knockers' the collections of sticks they saw carried into a horse-cab at Wimbledon station for transport to the windmill beneath which was the clubroom of the London Scottish club. And occasionally a golfer would greet with an infuriated glare, instead of the hoped-for tip, the smiling Cockney running up to him, ball in hand, and shouting: "Ere y'are, guv'nor. I fielded 'im.' But gradually familiarity bred tolerance and then some understanding, particularly when men and boys looking for casual work discovered that the peculiar chaps called golfers were willing to pay for having their clubs carried and the ball hunted down in the rough.

The magazines of the time poked fun in various ways, and the most extravagant cartoons were not far removed from the truth. Picnics had been spread on putting greens, and boys had played cricket. Mothers were known to wheel perambulators across fairways, deaf to the shouts of 'Fore!' and blind to the risk of injury. There were also many cases of vandalism, by damage to greens and thefts of flagsticks and other accessories. Yet the very fact that people were taking notice of golfers, by sketches, by articles, and even by antipathy, meant that the game was becoming well known to the community at large. The effect was most marked on the middle-class residents near the places used for golf. From mere curiosity they proceeded to deep interest, then to the desire for participation. The wish was easily gratified for those who could be accepted as members of the few existing clubs, but there were severe limits on the number of vacancies. The ordinary business or professional man, tied to his particular suburb and with free time only at week-ends, found it difficult to satisfy his desire, and the answer had to be found in the construction of courses on private land and in accessible places. So the beginning of the 1890s saw the start of a great expansion of the golfing population, and the time was ripe for the development of inland suburban golf.

CHAPTER 9

Lords and Commons

During the last two decades of Victoria's reign golf changed its character while extending its boundaries. For centuries it had been virtually confined to Scotland and was as strange to the world at large as shinty and hurling are today for anyone except Irishmen. But in the 1880s it began to be a social attribute, cultivated and exploited by those who wanted to be and remain fashionable. The game now ranked with hunting, shooting and fishing as a pastime of the upper classes, and in the wake of this general enthusiasm for an interesting and absorbing novelty came the development of an important industry. Before 1885 there was little indication of any significant increase in the number of courses and golfers in England, yet ten years later the game was swinging along and gaining in momentum. It is impossible to point with any certainty to any particular reason for the spurt, but one who must have had much to do with it was the Rt Hon. Arthur James Balfour. Britain's future Prime Minister, eldest son of an East Lothian laird and brought up in a golfing atmosphere, was one of the most prominent politicians of the day. In 1887, aged only thirty-nine, he was appointed Secretary of State for Ireland by his uncle Lord Salisbury, the Premier, and immediately found himself in the public eye. No post in that government was less of a sinecure. Ireland was a cauldron of unrest, and the political situation sufficiently critical for Mr Balfour to be given the protection of detectives, who shadowed all his movements, even on his frequent rounds of golf at North Berwick and in London. North Berwick became a focal point for society sportsmen during the long vacation, and other Scottish resorts like Dornoch, Nairn and Lossiemouth shared in the benefits accruing from this new-found enthusiasm of the English. (Another golfing Prime Minister was Winston Churchill, pictured in Plate 6.)

People who enjoyed golfing holidays naturally wanted to play at other times, and demanded courses which would be accessible from the centres of cities or situated conveniently on the outskirts of country towns. One of the important effects of Mr Balfour's addiction to golf was a growing interest shown by his fellow-politicians. Members of both Houses at Westminster found the London commons— Mitcham, Tooting, Clapham and Wimbledon—most convenient for snatching an hour or two of golf during the Parliamentary sessions. Clapham was the nearest to Westminster but no golf was permitted there after 9.30 a.m. Tooting was also becoming restricted by building, but Mitcham was a very desirable site, situated in open country and having a gravel subsoil providing ideal conditions, even in winter. The attractions of Mitcham were exploited by the establishment of Prince's Golf Club in 1890, the prime mover being a leading local resident, Henry Deeley. Later he changed his name to Mallaby-Deeley, became an MP in 1910 and was made a baronet in 1922. But even in 1890 he was a man of substance and influence and, as Chairman of the Mitcham Common Conservators, well placed to further the project. His proposals for a club had the enthusiastic support of Mr Balfour and the Earl of Chesterfield and other parliamentarians, and Prince's Mitcham soon became a favourite course for Lords and Commons. A natural sequel was the institution of Prince's Ladies' club with a separate course and clubhouse on another part of the common.

During the next twenty years the love of golf was to spread beyond the upper classes, but in 1890 there was no breath of the wind of change. Mitcham was where the Lords and Commons and their ladies went to play golf, as did the socialites of Mayfair and Belgravia. Nothing could be more convenient. There was a railway station a few yards from the clubhouse, served by frequent trains from Victoria, and in less than half an hour after leaving the West End one could be treading the short springy turf so rare in the London area and breathing the fresh air of the yet unspoiled countryside. At first there was little interference from the public, for the local inhabitants were allowed to play at certain times, and the formation of the Mitcham Village Club in 1907 did not at first affect the situation. Then local feeling, spurred by democratic ideas, led to a change. The villagers took legal action to secure public playing rights on the common, and that was the beginning of the end for Prince's.

The development had been foreseen by Mallaby-Deeley and his

associates, and in 1904 he began to plan a similar project on the shores of Sandwich Bay, next door to Royal St George's. In June 1907, the Prince's Golf Club, Sandwich, was opened by Mr Balfour driving the first ball in the Founders' Gold Vase competition. During the next few years the strength of the Mitcham villagers grew steadily, and in 1924 the course became public under a deed of trust by which Prince's Golf Club Company Ltd made over to trustees the course and clubhouse and all other property of the club. In the following year the Mitcham Public Course was formally opened by the Labour Prime Minister, Ramsay Macdonald, and the metamorphosis was complete. No need to weep over the supplanting of the Lords and Commons by the commoners and villagers. The former went happily to the heathlands of Surrey, Sussex and Berkshire, or to the coast at Sandwich, Rye and Littlestone. The latter rejoiced in the untrammelled use of a fine course at their doorsteps. Life was hard at first because the trust was not endowed, but the Mitcham golfers have shared in the prosperity experienced by all public courses since 1946.

The golf at Mitcham in the 1890s was good, but the lack of privacy there and at other open spaces sent golfers further afield, looking for something more exclusive. One of the most important steps was taken in 1893 by a group of London barristers and judges, who founded the Woking Golf Club in a beautiful heathland setting about twenty miles from London. The membership is now drawn from a wider field although still with a strong legal character, but the importance of Woking is that it was the first of many great courses in Surrey and neighbouring counties which lie on heathland useless for agriculture but ideal for golf. Worplesdon and West Hill, Woking's near neighbours, began only fifteen years later and were preceded by Sunningdale, Burhill and Walton Heath. St George's Hill, Wentworth and the Berkshire were great heathland courses made shortly before or after the Great War. In the 1890s some golfers were able to find homes nearer London. The Richmond club started in 1891 in a secluded park near the Thames-side village of Ham, and with a beautiful old mansion as clubhouse. In the same year the West Middlesex club was founded on gravel soil at the side of the Uxbridge Road at Hanwell. In 1895 golfers at Kingston-upon-Thames obtained permission to lay out holes in the Home Park of Hampton Court, although no bunkers were allowed in case the grazing sheep fell into them. But wherever they went golfers tended to get away from the city.

Similar developments took place in the provinces. The Robin Hood, Moseley, Harborne, Handsworth and Edgbaston clubs were all formed in the Birmingham area before 1900, although Edgbaston, started in 1896, had to move outwards to a new site ten years later. The Anson club, one of the first to be formed in the Manchester Area, apart from Old Manchester, no longer exists, and the Trafford club, which played on nine holes adjoining the Lancashire County Cricket Club, also became a casualty of development. But the Manchester and Fairfield clubs, formed in 1882, remain, as does North Manchester (1894). The four Leeds clubs of the nineteenth century are still in existence, and there have been few casualties in the Liverpool area. The lease of the New Brighton Club, formed in 1899, ran out ten years later, but other clubs on the Wirral Peninsula, including Leasowe, Wallasey and of course Royal Liverpool are still flourishing, and the golfing grounds north of Liverpool remain as rich as ever. From the 1890s onwards golf, although no less a game for the lords, was becoming more and more a game for the commons.

The suburbs of Britain's big cities were becoming populated by social climbers—doctors, lawyers, dentists who practised among near neighbours, and merchants and bankers who travelled to and from their offices. This represented a marked change from custom, because for centuries the typical town had been indiscriminately both dormitory and work-place. The tradesman lived over his shop and the doctor over his surgery. The banker went upstairs from his counting-house after locking up the safe and sending his clerks to their attics. The merchant slept almost within reach of the bolts of cloth he handled during the day. But the development of industry and finance and the increasing prosperity of the middle classes combined to bring about great changes in the latter part of the nineteenth century. The city was no longer attractive for living, and families began to move away from the centre towards the perimeter. Rows of not unpretentious villas were occupied by rising folk striving to be better than their neighbours. All classes were increasing their importance relative to each other, and their standard of living. The best sites on hilly ground or on the banks of rivers were selected for the most commodious and elaborate dwellings, and the speculative builder was active in the nondescript area between. The game of social self-importance was now in full swing among the middle classes and the modes of Mayfair were followed by worldly men and their ambitious wives. To have a carriage and pair was a signal mark of distinction. To belong to the tennis club, act as sidesman in church, do good works, give parties, be 'at home' on certain days to acceptable callers, were habits essential to dwellers in the new suburbia, and so the social climbers lived in minuscule fashion the lives of those in high society whom they envied and imitated. To such people golf seemed to be a pastime peculiarly suitable for inclusion in the daily whirl, and membership of a golf club a useful addition to one's self-importance.

Golfers were known to come from privileged and moneyed classes, therefore golf must be included in the week-end activities. So in various parts of the country residents of equal standing combined to form clubs from which they hoped to derive not only health-giving exercise but also the right kind of social intercourse. Another advantage derived from such enterprises was the opportunity they gave for the establishment of exclusive rights, again in imitation of the upper classes. Many of the golf clubs started by society folk were closed to those regarded as outsiders. The phrase 'Visitors must be introduced by and play with a member' recurred in the details of such clubs published in the guide-books of the time, and there was no chance of entry to the course, let alone the club, for the stranger lacking the support of a member. A few clubs still operate in this way, but they are relics of a past which can never be recalled. In the 1890s they represented a large proportion of the existing clubs, and this prevented many would-be golfers from obtaining facilities. The only recourse was to self-help, and in this way middle-class private enclaves were established which were also protected by rules excluding those deemed inferior in class.

The new golfers, who rapidly became the majority, ran their clubs on modest lines, being well content with facilities on a par with those in the villas they occupied. And although they were careful to preserve the privacy of their courses at busy times, by charging higher green fees at week-ends or limiting week-end visitors to those playing with members, they were ready to provide play for mid-week strangers and arrange fixtures for visiting societies. Green fees became in time one of the most important features of the average club balance sheet. It needed little business acumen to realize that, to keep the club solvent without increasing subscriptions unduly, it was essential to use the course to the utmost. Societies were particularly welcome because, apart from the revenue produced in green fees, they contributed to the catering and bar receipts and helped to publicize the club.

Land, even on the outskirts of cities, was cheap and plentiful, and very soon golfers in various neighbourhoods were co-operating in the purchase or renting of suitable hundred-acre sites, and laying out courses. In this way they obtained all they desired—play-grounds exclusive to members and accepted visitors, and near enough to their homes to give them evening and week-end golf without expensive and time-consuming travel. The development had one particularly significant effect. It produced the typical suburban club, an association of local people belonging to various classes and interests who, brought together by golf, formed a social group which gained in quality and force by being heterogeneous. Doctors, parsons, shopkeepers, professors, artists and business men were all attracted to a game which provided exercise, fresh air, recreation and social intercourse, and from 1890 onwards there was a steady increase in the number of such clubs started in the environs of cities and towns all over England and Wales. In London alone the number of clubs within fifteen miles of Charing Cross rose from nine before 1890 to forty-nine by 1899. In the next decade this figure had almost doubled to eighty-nine, a nine-fold increase in two decades. And whereas all the pre-1890 clubs played on common land, practically all those founded subsequently had private courses.

The accelerated growth of clubs and courses in the Edwardian era was due mainly to a new type of ball which proved to be an even greater stimulant than the guttie had been fifty years earlier. In 1899 an American, Coburn Haskell, invented a ball composed of elastic wound at tension round a rubber core. The idea went through various stages of development and was introduced to Britain, where it met with scepticism and suspicion until, in the Open Championship of 1902, Sandy Herd used it and won the title. Herd was a fine golfer in the front rank and would no doubt have won in any case, but the fact that he used a rubber-core ball was decisive, and in a very short time the guttie became a museum piece. The new ball was easier to hit, livelier in behaviour and, most important of all, travelled longer distances. Golf had become much easier to play and consequently more popular, but popularity produced other problems by intensifying the need for more playing space.

Seclusion was probably the outstanding quality of most of the courses thus created in the suburbs. The majority would not have attracted golfers accustomed to playing on seaside links or downland. They were often laid out on clay soil in comparatively flat meadowland or parkland. The natural hazards were not exciting, being mainly hedges, ditches and trees, and there was no natural sand scooped out by the wind to form bunkers. But as bunkers were regarded as essential, the suburban designers made them by digging holes, piling the excavated earth to form banks, and filling the holes with sand. As sand was imported and fought a constant and losing battle with the underlying clay, maintaining bunkers was costly in labour and materials. When it is realized that a grassy hollow left rough will usually be a more difficult hazard than a sand bunker, it is difficult to understand why so much deference is still paid to the artificial hazard as a pale imitation of the real thing.

Many of the least suitable courses laid out before the Great War eventually disappeared under bricks and mortar, leaving no aesthetic regrets behind them. But they served their purpose in providing golf on the doorstep for many golfers who, lacking such facilities, would either not have adopted the game at all or would have found their enjoyment marred by infrequent and awkward journeys. In time many of them did have to go further afield, for as the big cities grew and buildings took the place of green countryside, so new sites had to be found beyond the spreading tide of bricks and mortar. Since these necessary changes were accompanied by an increase of leisure, the introduction of the five-day week, the development of dormitory towns and, above all, the popularity of the motor-car, the situation of the golfer was no worse. Indeed, it was much better, because in most cases the new sites were more suitable, and modern ideas about design and construction combined to make the courses pleasing and natural in appearance.

CHAPTER 10

Enter Madame

A survey of four or five centuries has so far lacked a reference to women's golf, for the good reason that the nineteenth was more than half over before the ladies began to take an active part, even in Scotland. Many more years were to pass before they established themselves as capable, within physical limitation, of emulating their menfolk on the links. History is not entirely mute on women golfers in the feather-ball days, but the recorded incidents are isolated. In 1565 Mary Queen of Scots incurred the criticism of her enemies for 'playing golf in the fields by Seton' too soon after the death of Darnley, her husband. From our knowledge of the clothes and customs of the time it must be assumed that the exercise was limited to small strokes along the ground. Nearly 250 years later, in 1810, the Musselburgh Golf Club subscribed for a creel to be won 'by the best female golfer who plays on the annual occasion on 1st. Jan next . . . to be intimated to the Fish Ladies by the Officer of the Club'. There is no record of a previous or later competition for fishwives, and it is probable that the contest for New Year's Day 1811 was suggested as part of a programme of fun and games to celebrate 'the annual occasion'.

It is clear that in 1810 and for many years afterwards golf was considered unsuitable for women, that few of gentle birth played at all before about 1860, and that many more years passed before they progressed beyond the discreet and ladylike movements associated with chipping and putting. Yet before the end of the century the Ladies' Golf Union had been formed, championships decided, and women in all parts of Britain were swinging the club, if not with abandon at least without fear of being thought immodest. This fairly rapid change in convention was the result of relaxation of early Victorian taboos, the development of female emancipation, and above all the gradual disappearance of voluminous and restrictive clothing fashions—the crinoline and the bustle. For the greater part of the nineteenth century the opinion that golf was not a game for women was based not only on the prejudice against feminine participation in exercises involving muscular effort and unseemly attitudes, but also on the general assumption—by men— that a woman's place was in the home. Her chief concern was to be a perfect hostess and manager of the household, an efficient producer and raiser of children, and a companion for her husband, particularly in the role of patient listener to his tales of exploits on the links.

Over the years the 'golf widow' has been a subject for satire and an object of sympathy, but the conventional picture of the poor neglected spouse waiting at home for the return of her lord and master, full of bonhomie and claret, flushed as much by the wine taken at dinner as by the day's exertions, is very wide of the mark. The 'little woman', on the contrary, was glad to have her menfolk out of the house and so unable to interfere with the smooth running of the home and the social pursuits, mainly of a sedentary character, with which she occupied her leisure hours. If the well-born or well-to-do ladies of the time had their thoughts turned to pastimes out of doors, a gentle game of croquet was about the limit of their aspirations, or indeed of their capacity, tight-corseted as they were and clothed in floor-length dresses over layers of petticoats.

In 1860 there was no hint of feminine intrusion on a purely masculine domain, but the seeds of revolution were already being sown. Robert Clark, the Edinburgh bookseller and author of the classic *Golf: A Royal and Ancient Game*, published in 1875, wrote (page 69):

> Of late years the Ladies, as an improvement on such drivelling games as croquet and lawn billiards, have taken vigorously to golf, and the Ladies' Green at St. Andrews is now a very charming feature of the place. . . . The skill of the fair competitors is by no means to be despised, and *on their own ground* [my italics] the best of them would be backed freely against the cracks of the R. and A.

This was a hyperbolic reference to the Ladies' Putting Club, founded on 5 September 1867, and using at first a piece of ground on the seaward side of the Royal and Ancient clubhouse not far from the present Ladies' Putting Course which one crosses or skirts on the way to the first tee of the New Course. In 1860 Mrs Robert

Boothby, whose husband was a scratch member of the R. and A., began to 'play golf' with a few other ladies on some waste ground behind Gibson Place, near the railway station. The caddies had made a few 'holes' where they played in their spare time, and the ladies took advantage of this ready-made 'course', but were embarrassed by the presence of men and boys who no doubt made derogatory remarks about ladies taking to golf, even putting. Mr David Burie, an R. and A. member, said the Gibson Place area was too public for them, and promised to look out for a nicer spot. He found one near the R. and A. clubhouse, and the move was quickly followed by the formation of a club. Mr Burie volunteered to be manager and secretary, Mrs Robert Boothby was elected President, and a small sum fixed for subscriptions, sufficient to pay for someone to maintain the holes—probably not much more work than would have been involved in caring for a lawn. The opening meeting was held on 5 September 1867, and in the following November the first challenge trophy—a St Andrews cross made from pebbles—was played for.

Soon afterwards the ladies had a shock. They were preparing for a competition when a man arrived, on the orders of the landowner, Captain Cheape, forbidding them to use the ground unless they paid for it. Their case was taken up by R. and A. members and an agreement was reached with Captain Cheape for the ladies to pay £7 a year rent. The R. and A. members promptly chose a still better part of the ground, and the Ladies' Putting Club became established on the present site.

The interest in these activities shown by R. and A. members was indicative of the gradual erosion of the age-old idea that golf was not a game for women. Mrs Boothby must have been a powerful influence in this direction, but the whole climate was changing. The passive role was being abandoned and a more active part played by women no longer content to be onlookers. In 1792 the Gentlemen Golfers of St Andrews took the unprecedented step of holding a '*fête champêtre*' for the ladies' during the week of the October meeting. The innovation must have been welcomed on all sides, for a minute dated four years later records a decision to play for the silver club on 5 October and to 'have a Ball on the Friday as usual'.

It was probably with something of the same condescending indulgence that the R. and A. members, three-quarters of a century later, encouraged their ladies in their desire to 'play golf', but they were not to know that by the hundredth anniversary of that *fête champêtre* women golfers would be playing round the Old Course of St Andrews and testing their skill on many other full-length courses throughout the land. For the foundation of Scotland's first women's golf club antedated by only one year a similar enterprise in England. In 1868, only four years after the formation of the Royal North Devon club, the ladies of that neighbourhood formed their own organization. The Westward Ho! and North Devon Ladies' Golf Club, to give its full original title, was a go-ahead body from the start, with 47 founder members to whom were added 23 members of the men's club as associate members. There was no question then, nor for a long time to come, of playing on the main course. The crinoline, elaborate, commodious and unwieldy, was fashionable from 1850 until the late 1870s, and even then the less graceful bustle did little to relieve women from the inhibitions of cumbersome fashions. These made them attractive in the drawing-room but rendered impossible any attempt at athleticism out of doors. In addition the ladies of Westward Ho! had to submit to masculine control of their affairs. A small course was laid out for them on spare ground near the Pebble Ridge, and it was a rule that 'no other club shall on any account be used on the Ladies' Course besides a wooden putter'. Moreover the course could be used only every other Saturday from 1 May to 31 October. The North Devon pioneers, in fact, were as far away as their sisters in St Andrews from the pleasures of real golf. A sketch published in the *Graphic* some time in 1873 and reproduced here as Plate 2 shows members of the Westward Ho! ladies' club in a competition. A bell tent stands in the background and the scene is one of general liveliness, with one maiden indelicate enough to have raised her putter to shoulder height. The foreground is full of youth and beauty and old-fashioned courtesy. One lady, dressed in dark-coloured and flounced satin from neck to ankles and wearing an enormous bonnet, is putting while a gentleman in tail-coat and bowler hat, with a card in one hand, bends forward to encourage her. A young lady, also flounced and frilled, stands just behind with a putter, having evidently just missed holing out with her own ball, which lies on the lip of the hole.

This picture pinpoints the limitations imposed on women golfers a hundred years ago, and the early enthusiasm of the Westward Ho! ladies was not proof against frustration. Although the club was successful enough at the start for the flags to be placed in the holes every Saturday instead of fortnightly, the club became dormant in 1878 and, when revived in 1890, attracted only twenty-four members. By this time women were venturing on to proper golf courses and using many more clubs than the putter. The second oldest ladies' club in England, the Ladies' London Scottish, was formed in 1872 as a branch of the men's club and became in due course the Wimbledon Ladies' Club, following the schism. The members played on the common but they were not free agents. One rule stipulated that all the members of the men's club were to be deemed honorary members and could even play in the ladies' competitions, although not allowed to take prizes. The men's club also exercised general supervision and had two seats on the committee. It is clear that the men at that period were far from enthusiastic about women taking up the game, and sceptical of their ability to achieve anything worthwhile, either as players or as administrators. Time was soon to prove them wrong.

CHAPTER II

The first English professionals: 1870 onwards

Only three years after its foundation the North Devon Club became Royal North Devon when, in 1867, the Prince of Wales consented to be patron. A few years later golf had become so popular there that a resident professional was appointed —Johnny Allan from St Andrews, who very soon afterwards brought his brothers Jamie and Matt from Scotland to share in the work. They were all good players of championship standard and therefore played a great deal among themselves and with members, but, like all professionals in those days, they had plenty of work making and repairing clubs and balls, and maintaining the links. The Allans, first professionals to serve an English club, were Scots, and neither then nor for many years afterwards was there any prospect of getting an Englishman to fill such posts. Yet an English school was in the making and it was at Westward Ho! that the first steps in golf were taken by one destined to be the original leader of that school—John Henry Taylor, the first English-born professional to win the Open Championship.

Son of a Northam labourer and made fatherless while still at school, Taylor helped the family income by working as a houseboy at various houses, including the family home of the Hutchinsons. When Horace Hutchinson came down from Oxford for the vacations he often had Taylor for his caddie, and this was the lad's introduction to the game which was to be his livelihood. As was customary in those days he learned by competing with other caddies in the intervals between rounds, on a rough 'course' behind their shed. They often made illicit use of their masters' clubs, left in their care, and imitated their styles and methods, not always with happy results. But Taylor, who modelled his style on that of Johnny Allan, soon outstripped his companions. When the Northam Working Men's club was formed in 1888 he was given a handicap of scratch, which did not prevent him from winning the first competition. He was then seventeen and working on the course as one of the green-keeping staff, but his days as an artisan-amateur were numbered. In 1891, just before his twentieth birthday, he was engaged as greenkeeper-professional by the Burnham and Berrow club, which had just started on a wild rabbit-infested waste of sand-hills on the Somerset shore of the Bristol Channel. Two years later Taylor made his first appearance in the Open championship and twelve months afterwards was crowned Champion at Sandwich—the first of his five victories.

The second non-Scottish professional to make his mark was Harry Vardon, Jersey-born, who succeeded Taylor as Champion in 1896. From then onwards the growing power of English golf was deployed successfully. On the field of play the Scots more or less held their own, but it is significant that although in the twenty-one years from Taylor's first victory to Vardon's sixth and last in 1914 the title was won seven times by Scots, all those winners were attached to English clubs. James Braid, five times champion, was at Romford, Essex, when he won for the first time in 1901, and later went to Walton Heath, Surrey. Jack White, the winner in 1904, was at Sunningdale, and Alexander Herd at Huddersfield. The last home-based Scot to win the Open was Willie Auchterlonie of St Andrews in 1893, and the reason for the subsequent sterility was basically economical. As soon as golf became popular in England the best Scottish professionals were lured over the Border by more attractive appointments, particularly in London and the Home Counties, which held the majority of affluent and influential golfers and the choicest selection of wealthy clubs. But the difference was not only of money. Few professionals living in Scotland were attached to particular clubs. Many of them were freelances, often following trades outside the game, and therefore gaining at best an uncertain living from golf. Engagement with an English club, on the other hand, meant settled employment, a shop of one's own, and a distinct circle of members to be served. The land of promise was not all honey—even the best jobs carried very small retaining fees, rarely as much as £1 a week and often far less, and the professional was expected to rely for most of his income on work in the shop, giving lessons, and playing with members. The most enterprising and business-like did well; but there were many less fortunate, most of whom had started as caddies and were installed in little workshops attached to the back regions of the club-house or tucked away in some obscure corner.

In the 1890s a professional was essential to the life of a golf club, the members depending on him for supplying gear and repairing breakages. Hickory shafts often split, as did the heads of wooden clubs. Iron heads worked loose and grips and whippings, despite wax and varnish, required attention from time to time. The professional and his assistants or club-makers were kept busy making new clubs, copying old favourites, and remoulding and repainting golf balls. Recruits to the game needed tuition, older hands occasionally had to be 'put right', and the professional was much more in demand for playing with members than is the case today. For the majority of the professionals, rounds with members were almost the only opportunities for actual play, and regular competition in the best company was impossible except for the privileged few who were successful enough to be able to leave their shops in safe hands and employ club-makers. The élite were often in demand for playing exhibition matches at other clubs, and easily obtained leave to take part in the few tournaments then promoted. But matches and tournaments were brief interludes in a working life bounded by the walls of a shop and the perimeter of the home course.

The average professional was the servant of the club and expected to work almost from dawn to dusk, which in summer meant very long hours. His shop was opened in time to welcome the first player of the day and did not close till the last member had left. Some idea of the amount of trading and work involved in making a shop profitable may be gathered from the prices charged by professionals in the 1890s. A typical list quotes a maximum of 6s. for a top-class club, 1s. for a best quality ball, 6d. for a remoulded ball, 2s. for a new hickory shaft and 2/6d. for a new clubhead. So much work was required in making a club that it is difficult to believe, even allowing for the differences in the value of money, that it was possible to get a good living from the process. The club-maker took a square-sectioned length of hickory and with plane, spoke-shave, file and glasspaper shaped it into a round-sectioned shaft, carefully tapered to give the right amount of whip in the right place—factors which varied according to the type of shaft and the wishes of the customer. There were no jigs with master-models for making club-heads from factory-sawn persimmon blocks. The worker cut a piece from the plank, used a saw to get some approximation to the desired shape, and then worked with an assortment of rasps, files, glasspapers and varnish to achieve the finished article. Allowing for the cost of materials, workmen's wages, and other items, it would seem that a professional in those days had to work very hard indeed for a decent living. But all things are comparative. The average wage of a mechanic then was twenty or thirty shillings a a week, membership of a good club cost only £2 or so per annum, and £500 a year was considered a very good income, with income tax not oppressive and surtax unknown.

The leading professionals included some who performed with distinction as players and others who with shrewd business heads, manual skill and capacity for improvement, built up reputations as providers of equipment, designers of courses, and general operators on the business side of the game. Some, like Taylor, had expert partners in their various undertakings. At the other end of the scale was the lowly professional-greenkeeper-steward in an out-of-the-way club with a small and not over-rich membership. For a small retaining fee, often only a few shillings a week, and perhaps a cottage, he would be expected to keep a shop, look after the course, and serve behind the bar, with his wife cooking and serving meals for the members. He was often an underpaid Pooh-Bah, with hands equally accustomed to planing a shaft, pushing a mowing-machine or tapping a beer-barrel. In some cases he did not even have full benefit from his shop-keeping, for there were clubs which claimed the profits from ball sales, although that iniquity was soon stamped out.

Between those extremes the great body of professionals, who would expect to average from £150 to £250 a year from their activities, with exhibition match fees and a few tournament prizes as bonuses, made a reasonable living. They worked hard and long to earn their money, but the job was congenial in many ways, providing a healthy active life and associations, however distant, with people of superior birth and social standing. Professionals were in general respected, if not accepted as equals, by the members, and even those who gained only a modest living were better off than if they had remained caddies or stayed in the various trades to which some of them had been apprenticed.

There was a clear social distinction between the professional of the 1890s and the members he served. He was not allowed to enter the clubhouse except through the back door. Only on the course and in his shop did he approach even slightly towards familiarity with his clients, and while his opinion on golfing matters was often canvassed and usually respected, he was neither tempted nor encouraged to overstep the conventional boundary. Nevertheless, the life of a golf professional appealed to many who had started life in lowly station, and had acquired knowledge and skill, even if sometimes by rough-and-ready methods. The majority lacked polish, but those gifted with native commonsense and who exercised self-discipline found their rewards in popularity for themselves and the trust of those they served. And it cannot be denied that as the twentieth century approached, the professional was recognized as member of a distinct class, superior to caddies, club-makers and hangers-on. In earlier days amateur golfers made no distinctions among those who served them. In places where the game was really a local industry, like St Andrews, there was no lack of experienced men ready to earn money by helping amateurs, and therefore no need for the appointment of a professional. But when golf was taken up by the English, circumstances demanded a different approach. As the guttie-ball revolution spread, each new club found it necessary to appoint someone who could teach and supply clubs and balls, and as demand outstripped the supply of Scots for such jobs, so Englishmen came forward to invade a hitherto Scottish preserve.

Statistics of the 1890s show clearly the rapid increase in the number of non-Scottish professionals. In 1889, when the Open Championship was played at Musselburgh for the last time, 34 of the 37 professionals competing represented Scottish clubs or centres, the remaining 3 being Scottish professionals attached to English clubs—Eastbourne, Coventry and Warwick. Four years later, at Prestwick, there were 27 entrants from Scottish courses and 16 from English clubs, the latter including 10 non-Scottish professionals. In 1894 the Championship was played in England for the first time, and of the 60 professionals at Sandwich only 14 were Scots representing Scottish clubs, 25 of the other 46 being non-Scottish. Comparisons between events played as far apart as Prestwick and Sandwich could be misleading, the one being as convenient for the Scots as it was inconvenient for the English, and the other having the opposite effect. But in 1897 Hoylake was a half-way point. Of the 69 professionals competing there, 17 entered from Scottish clubs and of the remaining 52 only 16 were Scots. From this near-equality between the races the following years saw a steady decrease in the proportion of Scots to other nationalities in the Championship, and this tendency must also have shown itself in the respective numbers employed throughout the United Kingdom.

CHAPTER 12

The establishment of women

For many years after the formation of women's golf clubs at Westward Ho!, Wimbledon and St Andrews any significant advance in that direction was inhibited by feminine fashions, Victorian ideas of propriety, and man's low estimate of women's ability to play real golf. The golfer's wife was not expected to play, but instead to lend an appreciative or sympathetic ear to tales of weal or woe, and to look suitably charming and engaging on the rare socio-golfing occasions, such as prize-givings or receptions, which required her presence. The following verse, written about 150 years ago, summarizes the situation perfectly:

> The game is ancient, manly, and employs
> In its departments women, men and boys.
> Men play the game, the boys the clubs convey,
> And lovely woman gives the prize away.

No doubt the cultured lady of early Victorian times was content to be a distant observer of the golfing scene and to venture there only for social purposes. Fifty years later, lovely woman was not disposed to restrict herself to giving away prizes. She had prize-winning ambitions of her own, and towards the end of the century began to satisfy them in a way which surprised and disconcerted men who had for so long believed that golf could never be a serious game for the other sex. For years they had been mildly amused, even scornful, about what they regarded as puny efforts to emulate the men. In the *Golf* volume of the Badminton Library, published in 1890, Lord Wellwood (later Lord Moncrief) put the masculine view (pages 47–8):

> We have always advocated a liberal extension of the right of golfing to women. Not many years ago their position was most

degraded. Bound to accompany their lords and masters to golfing resorts for the summer months, they had to submit to their fathers, husbands, and brothers playing golf all day and talking golf shop the whole of the evening, while they themselves were hooted off the links with cries of 'fore' if they ventured to appear there. We therefore gladly welcome the establishment of ladies' links . . . which have now been generously provided for them on most of the larger greens [courses]. Ladies' links should be laid out on the model, though on a smaller scale, of the long round [the full course], containing some short putting holes, some longer holes admitting of a drive or two of seventy to eighty yards, and a few suitable hazards. We venture to suggest seventy or eighty yards as the average limit of a drive, not because we doubt a lady's power to make a longer drive, but because that cannot well be done without raising the club above the shoulder. . . . The postures and gestures requisite for a full swing are not particularly graceful when the player is clad in female dress. As to the ladies playing the long round with men as their partners, it may be sufficient to say, in the words of a prominent young player who found it hard to decide between flirtation and playing the game: 'It's all mighty pleasant but it's not business'.

Some years earlier, a *Cornhill Magazine* article in 1867 described the reaction of a choleric colonel to the fact that one of his opponents in a foursome was accompanied by his wife and sister-in-law: 'The links is not the place for women, exclaimed the Colonel. They talk incessantly, they never stand still, and if they do the wind won't allow their dresses to stand still.'

Time also does not stand still, and Lord Wellwood had not moved with the times. When his article was published, young women were already demolishing his argument in a practical way. Horace Hutchinson, editor of the Badminton volume, must have been well aware of the phenomena. As an amateur player of note he had been brought into contact with several women players well able to tackle long shots on full-length courses and produce good scores. In his *Fifty Years of Golf* (1919) he recalled playing on the championship course at Prestwick with the sisters Molly and Sybil Whigham, members of a leading Scottish golfing family, and finding to his surprise that they could hit far enough to render the 'long course' a feasible proposition. He was even more surprised later, on visiting the Gloucestershire seat of Lord Eldon, to see Lady Margaret Scott competing on almost equal terms with her brothers Osmund, Denys and Michael, on a private nine-hole course. Many years later, in 1933 the Hon. Michael Scott, then a grandfather aged fifty-five, won the Amateur Championship. Fame came to his sister much earlier, for shortly after she had astounded Hutchinson by the ease with which she hit an unresponsive guttie ball from the turf with a brassie—a shot not easily achieved by the average man —she scored the first of three successive victories in the British Ladies' Championship.

Nevertheless, although the quality of these and some other exceptional women players was known to their intimate friends, the world of golf was still strongly masculine and mainly sceptical. Most men still did not consider the possibility of women's golf ever remotely resembling their own game. But even as Lady Margaret was perfecting her skill in Gloucestershire, great events were in train. In 1892 work started on two projects which at first were in opposition but quickly became fused—a national championship and a national ruling body for women. Dr Laidlaw Purves, of Wimbledon, who helped to start the Royal St George's club at Sandwich, had been campaigning for a national golf association for men which would organize and control a nation-wide handicapping system. The idea, which might have led to some other body than the Royal and Ancient Golf Club ruling golf, never progressed beyond discussion, but one practical outcome was the formation of the Ladies' Golf Union, in which Dr Purves and other Wimbledon golfers played a leading part in support of Miss Issette Pearson, the chief architect.

Some twenty ladies' clubs having promised support, a formation meeting was arranged to be held in London in April 1893. Meanwhile the Lytham and St Annes club in Lancashire had been planning a competition to produce a champion lady golfer. The Lytham project was made public shortly before the meeting called by Miss Pearson and her supporters and, since her plans naturally included a championship, the small world of women's golf was thrown into turmoil. Fortunately a compromise was reached with commendable speed. The meeting which formed the LGU agreed to hold the first championship at Lytham, and the trophy which that club had intended to provide was subscribed for by the founder clubs. What might have been a serious difficulty was overcome with no obvious signs of tears or temperament. The first championship was decided in June 1893, with thirty-eight entrants, and Lady Margaret beat Miss Pearson 7 and 5 in the final.

Although some Scottish players competed at Lytham, ten years elapsed before they had a championship of their own. This apparent conflict with the history of a game that had been almost exclusively Scottish for centuries can be explained by the fact that Scottish women started on no more than an even footing with their English sisters in the latter half of the nineteenth century. Furthermore, although the St Andrews Ladies' Putting Club had been in existence for many years, it was not until 1898 that the ladies of St Andrews formed a club for the purpose of holding competitions on the Old Course. They had been playing on the famous links for some years when the British championship was launched, and two of them, Agnes and Frances Grainger, had helped to form the LGU. In 1894 the sisters went to Littlestone for the second championship and thereafter worked enthusiastically towards organized golf for women in Scotland. In 1898 Agnes Grainger was the prime mover in a proposition, made and accepted at the annual meeting of the St Rule Club, a social club for ladies, that a golf club be formed from among the members. The entrance fee was fixed at half a crown and the annual subscription at ten shillings, and an ambitious programme of competitions was planned. Unfortunately the winter had started. Snow at the end of November caused postponement of the first competition, and when it took place a week later the weather was stormy and wet. In the circumstances the winning score of 108 net, returned by a Miss Bett with the help of a handicap of nine, was not at all bad, considering that in those days R. and A. medal winners were scoring in the mid-eighties. Miss K. Turner, one of the most skilful members, won the gold scratch medal a year later with 105, presumably in better weather. Her driving on that occasion was described as 'first-class', but her short game 'unequal', a type of frustration with which golfers have been all too familiar through the centuries.

Agnes Grainger was first chairman of the St Rule Ladies Golf Club, and her efforts to establish Scottish women's golf on a national basis bore fruit in 1903, when the first Scottish Ladies' Championship was played over the Old Course at St Andrews under the management of the St Rule club. In the following year the Scottish Ladies' Golf Association was founded by Agnes Grainger and Miss Hamilton-Campbell.

Golf for women was now fairly launched, and even men who had been most intolerant had to admit that women could play the game well and organize themselves. Indeed, since the LGU soon introduced a handicapping scheme and the men floundered along without one for the next thirty-five years, it may be thought that the ladies, outdriven on the links, were ahead in administrative ability. Before taking the final step the pioneers of the LGU consulted a number of prominent men golfers, and one who decried the whole idea did so with the best of motives, even if his actual words, in a letter to one of the founders, were uncompromising:

> Women never can unite to push any scheme to success. They are bound to fall out and quarrel. They will never go through a ladies' championship with credit or without tears. Constitutionally and physically women are unfitted for golf. They will never last two rounds of a long course in a day, nor can they hope to defy wind and weather. Temperamentally the strain will be too much for them.

Such views, so soon to be made ridiculous by events, were shared by the majority of the writer's fellow-men. Even the first LGU championship had to be decided over the Lytham Ladies' course of nine holes, because it was considered impossible for women to tackle the full-length course. The women at Littlestone, Kent, where the 1894 championship was played, also had their own separate nine-hole course, dubbed the 'hen-run', but the men of Littlestone perhaps had more tolerant ideas, or their ladies were more persistent and persuasive than those of Lytham. The Littlestone Ladies' club was founded in 1891 and from the start the members had freedom to play on the men's course at any time, so that course was used for the 1894 championship. Masculine interest in the event was almost confined to local members, but those who watched and possibly had come to scoff were converted on the spot by the spectacle of elegant ladies, clad in the ground-length wasp-waisted fashions of the period, not only raising the club above the shoulders but contriving to look quite graceful in such a posture. As for Lord Wellwood's seventy or eighty yards, there is no record of Lady Margaret's drives, but in the 1895 championship at Portrush, Northern Ireland, also won by Lady Margaret, a score of 89 by Sybil Whigham caused a sensation. In 1897 a driving competition was won by a competitor who achieved a carry of 133 yards (before the ball landed); and in 1899 Molly Whigham had complete drives (carry and run) of 214 yards and 234 yards at Westward Ho! All these were with the guttie ball, which had to be struck with shrewdness and good timing to produce a satisfactory result.

It is impossible for present-day players to imagine the difficulties caused for women golfers by the fashions of the time. The crinoline and bustle had departed in turn, but in their place were clothes which might have been designed specifically to prevent women from indulging in any sporting activity. Sleeves were so full-fashioned that elastic bands were worn to enable the player to see the ball on the tee as she swung upwards. The ample ankle-length skirts required a restraining band round the knees. The caps with scarves used by ladies in motor-cars were popular on the links. Blouses with stiff starched collars added to the general discomfort. The picture is terrifying enough when visualized in calm, fine weather. Rain and wind must have multiplied the difficulties ten-fold.

CHAPTER 13

Artisan golf in England

While the number of golfers in England and Wales grew steadily in the 1890s, they nearly all belonged to private clubs and there was little or no room for the working man who wanted to play. In most instances he could not even use the common-land courses which by that time were being maintained at the expense of the resident clubs who levied fees on visitors. The twin barriers to the progress of the working-class golfer were financial and social. Although the average club subscription of about £2 per year was small in comparison with the £50 of the present day, it represented more than a week's wages for the manual worker or labourer, and the expense of club membership did not end with payment of the subscription. The social barrier was even more difficult, for applications for membership had to be proposed and seconded and then approved by the existing members, and anyone not acceptable had no chance.

Circumstances were different in Scotland, where free golf had been enjoyed for centuries by everyone. It was not until 1913 that playing charges were levied for the use of the Old Course at St Andrews, and even then there were very low seasonal rates for St Andrews residents. England and Wales had no such tradition of free golf, yet there was a growing section of golfers virtually excluded from existing facilities. This situation was alleviated to some extent and in certain quarters by the start of a general artisan movement in 1897. A distinction must be drawn between this first real artisan club, the Cantelupe at Forest Row, Sussex, and some earlier organizations of working men. The St Andrews Mechanics' (later just St Andrews) Golf Club was founded in 1843 not to obtain playing privileges, which the members already had, but to enjoy social life and competitive activities. The Newbiggin-on-Sea

Mechanics, founded in Northumberland in 1885, and the Perth Artisans, started in 1887, were similar in constitution and circumstances. The Northam Working Men's Club, founded in 1888, played on Northam Burrows which, being grazing ground for the pot-wallopers, was open to all inhabitants. But there was an element of restriction there because members of the Royal North Devon Club paid for the upkeep of the course and therefore enjoyed a priority readily conceded by the working men, many of whom worked for Royal North Devon members.

While the members of private clubs denied playing rights to all outsiders save those properly introduced, there was a general wish, particularly in rural districts, to provide facilities for those who could neither afford membership nor be considered eligible. This gave rise to the artisan movement which soon became an important part of the golf scene. Arrangements varied from club to club but generally the artisans were allowed to play at certain times, particularly early morning and late evening, when members of the parent club were not active, and were expected in return to perform various tasks on the course. In some cases the artisans also paid a small fee. But whatever the precise conditions, they all relished the facilities provided, and the association with the parent clubs brought mutual benefits. The artisans built their own modest clubrooms or decorated and maintained huts allotted to them. They imposed small annual subscriptions on themselves, ran competitions and social functions, and soon exercised a significant influence. Their existence led to the production of good players who might otherwise have remained undiscovered. The Forest Row artisans, who took the name of Cantelupe, played on a course maintained by the Royal Ashdown Forest club, formed in 1889. In addition to providing free golf in return for work on the course the parent club made an annual grant. Foremost among the men of Cantelupe was Abe Mitchell, who turned professional in 1912 after reaching the final of the Amateur Championship and subsequently became a famous Ryder Cup player. He was originally a gardener and woodman, and in that work developed the wiry strength and steel-like wrists which made him the most powerful driver of his time. The star player in the Northam Working Men's club was J. H. Taylor, who won the Open Championship five times.

Artisans were dependent on the goodwill and interest of the parent club members, but this could be relied upon, particularly in the rural districts where most of the artisans lived and worked.

In many cases the initial steps were taken not by the artisans but by their benefactors. This could often have been good policy, since so much depends, in a small country community, on harmony and co-operation at all levels. Whatever the motives, the results in most cases were happy relationships between those who gave and those who received, and the artisan movement would not have grown so fast without the active encouragement of the privileged classes.

Soon after artisan golf began at Forest Row another Sussex Club, Crowborough Beacon, followed suit, the inaugural meeting being held in the clubhouse with Mr G. T. Langridge, a founder member of the parent club, in the chair. He announced that Lord de la Warr had agreed to be patron, and the new club was forthwith called De la Warr Artisans. During the next twenty years the artisan movement grew not only in the rural areas where the feudal spirit was still strong, but also in the big towns of the south. Progress was slower in the Midlands and the north, possibly due to regional differences in circumstances and outlook. A Village Play Committee established at Hoylake had two hundred members with limited playing facilities over the Royal Liverpool links; and at nearby Wallasey the West Cheshire Villagers played over the local links 'by permission'. It was inevitable that the continued increase of such clubs should lead to organization, and but for the War Britain would have had this before 1921, when J. H. Taylor was the moving spirit in the formation of the Artisan Golfers' Association, and became the first chairman. It was to be a very important body in British golf but its character changed with the changing social conditions in the country. Feudalism gave place to democracy, with predictable results.

CHAPTER 14

Professionals in business

The golf explosion of the 1890s had two beneficial effects on the condition of the average professional golfer: the number of jobs increased and the prospects improved. There was no significant change in the normal retaining fee, a nominal sum paid by a club to ensure that the professional ran a shop and provided services for members. The retainer was the base on which the professional built his business, and the new men included many who were able to expand their activities beyond the narrow limits prescribed by the requirements of their own members. Some of the early Scottish professionals, including Allan Robertson, Tom Morris and Willie Park, were better qualified than most of their contemporaries for making a good living from golf. But their efforts were surpassed by one who can be described as the first of the businessmen professionals, Park's son Willie Junior. He won the Open Championship twice and used that reputation as a springboard for various activities, the most important of which concerned the design and construction of courses. Brought up to be frugal in habits and careful with money, he was a shrewd man who, having taken easily to golf on a championship level, assimilated just as easily the art of exploiting success.

By playing many money matches Park kept his name before the public long after his championship victories had become history. This publicity and his flair for business brought him so much work at home and abroad that he established a London branch. He laid out many courses in the United States and Canada, having seen the immense possibilities in countries where golf was only beginning to be popular. He was also the first professional to produce a book on golf, published in 1896. He was then heavily engaged in many enterprises and for several years continued to prosper. But he died aged sixty, from what was generally believed to be the effects of overwork.

The idea that the activities of a professional and therefore his earning capacity were restricted to course maintenance, club-making, teaching and playing was dispelled so completely by Park that he soon had imitators, forming a generation of golfers who used their names and reputations to further their interests. John Henry Taylor was one of the first, and one of the most successful. In those days professionals graduated mainly from the caddie-shed or the club-maker's work-bench. The former, who included Taylor and Vardon, had little or no knowledge of club-making when they became professionals, but profited so much by their skill as players that they were able to employ club-makers. Their great rival James Braid, on the other hand, was a joiner by trade and played golf as an amateur until he took to club-making. Whatever Taylor lacked in that department—he once modestly confessed to inadequacy even in repairs—was supplied by his boyhood friend George Cann who, at about the time Taylor went to Burnham, was apprenticed to Charles Gibson, the Westward Ho! professional.

In 1894 Cann joined Taylor at Winchester and the partners began years of prosperous work supplying golf clubs to the world. Four years afterwards Cann went to the United States to open an American branch. Later still Taylor went into partnership with a leading golf course architect, Fred Hawtree, and here again the combination of playing reputation and technical expertise was successful. There were many other shrewd, capable men who played golf of championship calibre and also had great reputations as craftsmen—George Oke of Fulwell, Fred Robson of Addington, Willie Ritchie of Sunningdale, Jack White of Sunningdale, Ben Sayers of North Berwick, and George Gibson of Kinghorn (Fife) are among the best remembered. They all employed several club-makers and some expanded their workshops into small factories, trading overseas as well as on the home market. The day of the golf manager had not dawned. Professionals of the early twentieth century managed their own affairs but were opening the door to a golden future.

CHAPTER 15

Women liberated

Fewer than twenty clubs were concerned in the formation of the Ladies' Golf Union in 1893, and there were probably not more than two thousand women players in Britain. But the existence of a corporate body set in train a series of enterprising promotions. In 1894 an open meeting was held at Ashdown Forest in Sussex and an annual meeting inaugurated at the Ranelagh Club near Barnes Common. At that time Ranelagh and the Hurlingham Club at Fulham were the recognized sporting centres for London society, with polo as the principal attraction. Ranelagh's golf course, on the short side, meandering amidst ornamental trees and planned to avoid encroachment on the polo grounds, tennis courts and croquet lawns, was distinctive in lay-out and style. It was almost completely flat, and natural hazards were provided by yew hedges and the tall trees which cast their leaves on the grass each autumn. Ponds and statuary added to the variety of the shots demanded. Even the flagsticks were unusual, being topped by melon-shaped wicker baskets instead of the customary pennants.

Ranelagh's golf meeting, which included team contests and an international event, was a great occasion, and those who watched included many non-golfers interested, as society was in those days, in a new craze. The first Ladies' Championship in the previous year had caused considerable discussion, and the fact that the winner was daughter of a peer gave just that touch of glamour which helped to make golf for women not only respectable but also 'the thing to do'. Victorian snobbery was at its height and most of those who attended those early meetings, riding in family carriages and dressed in fashions most unsuitable for golf, did so mainly because it was 'Ranelagh'. This enthusiasm had a marked effect on the masculine attitude, because it was now obvious that women, although handicapped by their restrictive dresses, could play in the same style as men if not with the same power. Women's golf had made a startling advance from the days of chipping and putting, and the movement was in full swing. Many of the women's clubs started in the 1890s played on short nine-hole courses and their modest quarters were often small huts or cottages near the men's clubhouse. But as they came more into the public eye by performances in open meetings and championships, their clubs developed into sections of the men's clubs, with rooms reserved in the main building, and restricted playing facilities on the full course. Eventually a mid-week day was set aside for the ladies, when they had priority and men ventured at their peril. The week-ends were still reserved for men who, having worked all the week, were entitled to have the course to themselves on Saturdays and Sundays. It was conceded that women could play in the afternoons of those days in mixed foursomes, but that was usually the limit. This arrangement has persisted to the present day at most clubs, despite changes in social structure and habits. Many women golfers now work full time and are free only at weekends, but this has made little difference. The men's view was that women paid lower subscriptions for fewer privileges. They had their mid-week day and their week-end mixed foursomes and must be content. It mattered not that many business and professional women would gladly pay the full subscription and have equal rights, and that many tired business men take days off in mid-week.

Although the late Victorian male had to admit that women could play proper golf on a proper course, he tended to preserve some remnants of the old restrictions. The women could no longer be banished to their 'hen-runs' but they could be kept in their place. There were very few autonomous and independent ladies' clubs in the 1890s, and the subordination of the majority can be gauged from the following extract from the history of the Home Park club at Kingston-upon-Thames, *circa* 1896 (page 23):

> There was evidently strict control over the ladies. They were
> informed very early on that (a) they would be accountable to the
> Committee (of the men's club) at all times; (b) all notices put up
> on their board must be initialled by the Secretary before being
> posted; and (c) all communications must come through the
> Ladies' Advice and Suggestion Book, not verbally, and permission
> to make fixtures for medals and matches must be asked for in the
> said book.

No ladies' section or club nowadays would accept such restrictions, even if there were a men's club daring enough to apply them. But even in 1896 there were women golfers who pursued an absolutely independent path. Significantly enough they existed in the north of England, and one surviving to the present day is the Formby Ladies' club at Freshfield, near Southport. The Formby men's course is renowned as a fine test of golf which has been used for many important events, including the Amateur Championship. But inside the main circuit is the course of the Formby Ladies' club, expertly designed for the purpose. Formby Ladies started with a modest clubhouse costing about £300, which was enlarged in 1908. The course is leased from the men's club but the women manage their own affairs, employ their own green-keeping and catering staffs, and have their own equipment, furniture and machinery. Another and later example from the south of England is Sunningdale Ladies' club, with a course considerably shorter than that of Formby Ladies. It marches with the Old Course at Sunningdale laid out by Willie Park, but there is a separate woman-controlled clubhouse.

These are among the few exceptions to the general rule that women golfers, although running their own clubs so far as internal administration and social and competitive activities are concerned, depend on their respective men's clubs for catering, course maintenance and all other matters, including finance. This arrangement, essential in most cases for economic reasons, and also the best means of integrating the affairs of both sides, is rendered acceptable by changed social conditions. In Victorian times segregation of the sexes was the rule, and the men, in addition to discouraging women from playing on the full course, only grudgingly gave them space in the clubhouse. The move towards new attitudes was accelerated by the Great War, and soon it became desirable as well as possible for men and women to enjoy the game and its social activities in partnership. Lingering male prejudices remained. Sunday mornings were still sacrosanct to man. The mixed foursome was still relegated to the afternoon or evening. The stag party was not abandoned, but gradually became less important than the annual mixed dinner-dance. The most significant change was in the day-to-day social life. At one time ladies, if they drank at all, had a sherry in the lounge brought from the bar where the men unbent in masculine freedom. The next development was the mixed bar, which at first was usually a cubby-hole with a service hatch, a knock at which would bring the barman unwillingly away from his male customers. Today no club with lady members wishing to be up-to-date and solvent can afford not to make the mixed bar the largest and brightest room in the building, for that is often where the main business is done. Some clubs long ago gave up the pretence of male exclusiveness and the men-only bar in many cases has died of atrophy or survived tenuously as tray service for the few who eschew feminine company. So much has the world of golf turned on itself in the space of half a century. There are still clubs which exclude women entirely or admit them only on sufferance. But generally speaking the feminine invasion is complete and peaceful co-existence the order of the day.

Indeed it was from their own kind that women golfers encountered the greatest opposition to complete emancipation. Although many taboos had been thrown off, together with the unwieldy clothing of earlier days, certain rules of behaviour and deportment were observed in cultured circles, and the Ladies' Golf Union remained a bastion of the proprieties—at least in the field of championships and general competitive golf. When one recalls the jazz age and the antics of the bright young things in the 1920s it seems almost incredible that, prior to the British Ladies' Championship at Westward Ho! in 1933, no competitor had dared to appear on the course in anything but acceptable female costume. This meant skirts of decorous length, sleeved upper garments, and hats or bandeaux.

Before play began in that championship, the attention of golf journalists was diverted from the usual assessment of the chances of leading contenders to discussion of a rumour that a new and unknown entrant, a Miss Gloria Minoprio, would use only one club. There was much speculation as to her chances of winning even one hole, let alone a match, on such a links and with such a handicap. When she did appear the effect was shattering, for she wore a complete dark-blue outfit beginning with a turban-like woollen hat, descending to a high-necked close-fitting sweater and ending with a pair of exquisitely-tailored trousers with knife-edge creases. Reactions among the onlookers ranged from open admiration by the males to scandalized consternation among competitors and officials. The LGU reaction was immediate and predictable. A statement regretted 'this departure from the usual golfing costume', and the propriety of women's golf in the 1930s was emphasized by the players fully supporting this condemnation. Nevertheless a breach had been made and when, two or three years later, particularly wet and windy weather at the championship persuaded many competitors to wear macintosh trousers, not an eyebrow was raised nor criticism voiced. A few more years passed and Britain became involved in another war during which trousers became commonplace items in the feminine wardrobe. When championship golf was resumed in 1946 slacks were seen on the course in increasing numbers. Some rearguard actions were fought on the propriety front and Bermuda shorts, when they were introduced from America, were generally frowned upon and even banned in some quarters. But the ramparts were down for good and, a century after the ladies of Westward Ho! and St Andrews had made their first daring excursions into a man's world, women golfers were enjoying complete freedom. (Plates 2, 3 and 8 show some of these different clothing styles for women golfers from the 1870s to the 1930s.)

If anything were needed to emphasize the fulfilment of liberation it was provided at the 1974 business meeting of the Royal and Ancient Golf Club by a decision to throw open the R. and A. clubhouse, including locker-rooms and the main lounge, for the use of competitors and officials in the British Ladies' Championship of 1975.

When the Ladies Championship was played at St Andrews for the first time, in 1908, it was sufficient cause for comment that the Old Course was used for such an event. The R. and A. members of the time were courteous and helpful, providing referees and stewards, allowing the Ladies' Golf Union flag to be flown at their masthead, and even inviting the players to tour the clubhouse and inspect the historic trophies, under the guidance of the Captain, Lord Stairs. But the competitors had to use their hotels and boarding-houses for changing and eating, and it was much the same in 1929 and even on the third occasion in 1965. The decision of 1974 therefore indicated that in less than a decade masculine intolerance had retreated from the entrenchment of two centuries of tradition.

CHAPTER 16

America started late,
but . . .

The seeds of Scottish golf scattered all over the world during the last hundred years have rooted firmly and produced flourishing plants, but in greatest profusion in the United States. That growth was so virile and fruitful that there are now more golf courses and many more players in America than in the rest of the world together. The Americans took the simple Scottish game and transformed it into a sophisticated way of life indispensable to most classes. It has produced hundreds of great players, many new and enterprising ideas, and a luxurious milieu far removed from the humble sand dunes of East Scotland. The start of American golf was humble, too, but soon acquired a polish as money was poured into the game. Nevertheless, in that cosmopolitan atmosphere it spread to all sections of the community, so that today there are not only many expensive and exclusive country clubs in beautiful surroundings and exotic holiday courses on the coasts of Florida and California, but also hundreds of public courses which, although numerous in and near the big cities, cannot comfortably accommodate all who wish to play.

Nothing could have been less ostentatious than the start. John Reid, a New Yorker born at Dunfermline in Scotland, hankered in middle age for the game he had known in boyhood, and when one of his compatriots departed for a business trip to Britain, Reid asked him to obtain some clubs and balls at St Andrews. When they arrived Reid dug a few rough holes in a meadow and invited his neighbours to join him in a game most of them had never seen. He had struck a match and started a prairie fire. The idea that it would be interesting to hit a ball with a stick and walk after it was foreign to the general concept of sport in a virile new world, but it soon had converts among the uninitiated, and reawakened

enthusiasm in the hearts of many exiled Scots. The latter, led by
Reid, were the pioneers, but soon found themselves outstripped by
American-born converts. Reid's modest coterie became organized
as the St Andrews Golf Club in 1888, and progress was so rapid
that six years later there were enough clubs, some started on more
ambitious lines, to form the United States Golf Association.

The second oldest US club was founded in 1889 at Middles-
brough, Kentucky, but the most prestigious development was
activated by the exclusive circles of New York society and big
business. The present Newport Club on Rhode Island was started
in 1890 by a syndicate of millionaires including Theodore A.
Havemeyer, Cornelius Vanderbilt and John Jacob Astor. The idea
of golf as part of a wider social and sporting complex was exploited
for the first time when the exclusive Country Club at Brookline,
Mass., decided to add a golf course to the amenities. Meanwhile
Long Island, another holiday resort of the upper classes, came in
for attention, and the famous Shinnecock Hills club took shape in
1891. Golf reached the Middle West in 1893 when the country's
first full eighteen-hole course was laid out at Wheaton, Illinois.
This was the home of the Chicago Golf Club, brain-child of Charles
B. Macdonald, who had played golf while a student at St Andrews
and was to become one of the leading legislators in the USGA. The
prairie fire had now taken hold, but since golf required both time
and money, and young Americans were too busy using time to
make money, the development remained for some while largely in
the hands of the rich. The Long Island and Rhode Island millionaires did not hesitate to bring over Scottish professionals to design
courses, and they spared no expense in construction. For this
reason American golf in its early stages was almost as exclusive as it
had been in England before 1890. Then, as in England, the middle
classes became interested and created a more democratic situation.
The rich continued to be ostentatious and exclusive but their private playgrounds were soon greatly outnumbered by the American
equivalent of English suburban courses. For example, while the
Chicago Club's course, about twenty miles from that city, retained
its exalted status, by 1900 there were more than a score of clubs,
mostly on more modest lines, in the district. One inevitable result
was the emergence of a race of young American players destined to
take the golf world by storm. Many were introduced to golf by
working as caddies and became professionals. Later, with high
schools and colleges adopting golf as an essential part of their

sporting programmes, the amateur game grew equally strong.

Nevertheless, early American golf was dominated by British players. In January 1895 Horace Rawlins, aged nineteen, arrived from England to be assistant at the prestigious Newport (RI) club. In the following October the first official US Open Championship was played on Newport's nine-hole course, and Rawlins won by two strokes from Willie Dunn, the Scot who laid out the Shinnecock Hills course and was professional at that club. During the next fifteen years the title was won continuously by golfers from Britain, mostly Scots. They included Willie Smith and his brother Alex, two of many Carnoustie men who settled in the USA as teachers and players, and Willie Anderson of St Andrews, who won four times. Harry Vardon, who won in 1900, was neither immigrant nor Scot. Born in Jersey, Channel Islands, he was at the height of a great career, and holder for the third time of the British Open title, when he made an extensive tour of the United States. He impressed everyone by the polished style and power of his game, and unconsciously gained converts wherever he went. The Vardon message rang loud and clear in the hearts of many young Americans, one of whom, Johnny McDermott, became in 1911 the first home-born winner of the US title. He won again in 1912 but national enthusiasm received its biggest boost in 1913. Vardon and Ted Ray, then holder of the British title, had come over to play in the US Open, and it was generally expected that one or the other would win. But a Boston store-clerk of twenty, Francis Ouimet, who had learned the game as a caddie but continued to play as an amateur, astonished everyone by tying for first place with the two Englishmen, and then beating them soundly in the play-off.

Golf was now as much American as British, and, with the advantages of more space, a larger population, and profit from British experience, Americans carried the game to realms undreamed of elsewhere, even in the early twentieth century. Nevertheless, although millionaires were carving new courses out of the Californian desert with the help of expensive irrigation systems, and real estate developers were exploiting the southern and western coasts, the middle classes were even more active in and around the cities and big towns. Most of the inhabitants could neither afford nor qualify for membership of private clubs, and this started a vigorous trend towards the construction of courses which, whether owned by municipalities or profit-making companies, were open to all on payment of fees. This side of American golf reached such large proportions in a few years that in 1922 the USGA instituted the Amateur Public Links Championship, which attracted 140 entries. In the following year a team championship was included and drew four-man teams from eighteen cities. By 1938 the individual entry had risen to 248 and 55 cities were represented by teams. The meeting having become unmanageable in that form, sectional qualifying was introduced in 1939 and 2,401 players competed at 33 centres. The entry was a USGA record, twice as large as the average entry for the Amateur Championship and nearly 1,000 more than the average for the Open. At that period, if the British National Association of Public Golf Courses had promoted a team championship, it would have attracted no more than a dozen entries. This tremendous difference between the two countries was due mainly to the fact that America did not have many clubs of the British suburban type, with mixed memberships of professional and business men and tradesmen. Wealth and social standing could open the doors of the most exclusive clubs in the United States, and give access to the coastal playgrounds, but the average middle-class American had to have golf on his doorstep, and the demand was met by the builders of public courses. Later on, driving ranges and par-three courses, constructed to conserve space and accommodate the growing tide of golfers by night as well as by day, were added to the sporting amenities of the cities, and in this way public facilities met a need which, in Britain, had been satisfied largely by private suburban clubs.

America's women golfers, unlike their British sisters, came into a receptive masculine world. Eight years elapsed between the first British Amateur Championship and the first Ladies' Championship. In the United States the gap was little more than a month. The USGA Amateur Championship in October 1895 brought such quick reaction from the ladies that they promoted their own championship a few weeks later. It was contested by stroke play over eighteen holes, the thirteen competitors playing nine holes before lunch and nine holes afterwards. The winner, Mrs Charles Brown of Shinnecock Hills, scored 132. The 1896 championship, promoted by the USGA, was decided by match play after a stroke qualifying competition, and the new champion, seventeen-year-old Beatrix Hoyt of Shinnecock Hills, won the qualifying test with 95, which was 37 strokes better than Mrs Brown's score in the previous year. Miss Hoyt also became first holder of the present trophy, donated by a Scottish MP, Robert Cox of Edinburgh, who was visiting

America. Miss Hoyt was easily the best American woman golfer of her time, for she had the lowest qualifying score five years running and won the title three times. She and her contemporaries had the advantage of being encouraged and helped by men. American women suffered, like those in Britain, from incommodious garments, but not from masculine scepticism and intolerance.

CHAPTER 17

The real estate boom

From the start of suburban private golf to the opening of the Great War the paramount need was to accommodate a rapidly increasing number of golfers who required facilities within easy reach of their homes. Those who went to Westward Ho!, Sandwich and Hoylake and other seaside links were mainly men who could afford the time involved. But the new golfers of the 1890s came chiefly from the professional and commercial classes and, living within convenient reach of their places of work, naturally sought leisure facilities in the same neighbourhoods. A golf course therefore became a valuable amenity, but for various reasons often lacked quality. The choice of land was dictated by availability, price and accessibility rather than suitability for golf. Northam Burrows were 'destined by Providence' and the Royal North Devon course was made easily and by degrees on open land free of charges. Those who laid out the Royal St George's links at Sandwich used ground which, while admirable for their purpose, was useless for anything else. Golfers seeking to establish themselves in the environs of towns and cities were in a very different situation. It was possible to lease agricultural land quite close to population centres, and the cost of laying out a course depended on the character of the ground, the ambitions of the founders, and the cash available. Since the course was all-important and golfers were not then hankering after luxurious quarters, most of the early clubhouses were modest in design and size, more sophisticated than the original tin hut at Westward Ho! but unpretentious in comparison with those of half-a-century later. The early suburban golfers needed little more than a pavilion providing locker-rooms, a bar, a lounge and perhaps a small card-room—essentials with no hint of ostentation. The buildings were often made of wood, with corrugated iron roofs, and their impermanent appearance reflected the insecurity of tenure of the land on which they stood.

The farmer was being pushed out of the suburbs by building developments and the real estate speculator began to influence the future of community existence. He joined with architect and builder to create neighbourhoods peopled by well-to-do commuters of the business and professional classes, living in detached or semi-detached villas in pleasant semi-rural surroundings. Developers were not slow to see the potentiality of golf, and the pattern changed. In the 1890s suburbanites already established added a golf course which, because the houses were already there, was located on the fringe of the neighbourhood it served. The twentieth-century developers tended to make the course integral with the estate —the focal point instead of an adjunct. In a balanced estate with a variety of dwellings, ranging from detached houses in half-acre plots to semi-detached villas eight or ten to the acre, the most valuable properties adjoined the course, affording the advantages of pleasant views and easy access to the fairways. Since the course was the centre of attraction, it had to be of a quality satisfying to prospective purchasers, with an adequate clubhouse to match the exclusive tone of the neighbourhood. So the earlier wooden structures gave place to handsome brick or stone buildings, planned for the purpose, and providing all essentials for the social and playing activities of the members.

These new estates varied in size and quality according to localities. The more expensive and extensive developments usually took place some distance from the town centre, mainly because land was more plentiful and cheaper, the inhabitants were richer, and the possibilities more attractive for golfers. In many instances the estates were based on country mansions which became clubhouses. Among the best known today are Wentworth in Surrey, Moor Park in Hertfordshire, Mere Country Club on the Cheshire outskirts of Manchester, Addington Palace near Croydon, the Manor House Hotel course at Moretonhampstead in Devon, the Temple Newsam public course in Leeds, the Hartsbourne Country Club in Hertfordshire, and the Stoke Poges club near Slough.

Unfortunately a mansion built on a large scale to provide opulent living in the days of lavish entertainment and big staffs was rarely suitable as a clubhouse. Staffing and catering problems and the high cost of maintenance and the heavy burden of rates, combined to make many such places unwieldy and uneconomical. The trouble was alleviated if the building was of historic importance, for then part of the cost of upkeep was offset by government help. The practice of using the ample and otherwise useless spare space for offices and residential flats also helped to cover overheads. But the up-to-date view is that where demolition is possible and permissible, it is better in the long run to do away with the existing building and erect one designed for golf.

The courses named are preserved because they form part of exclusive estates or are maintained by local authorities, but the real-estate boom, while doing much for the development of inland golf, held the seeds of decay. The golf course was a valuable amenity because it enhanced the attraction of the houses offered for sale, but as the demand for dwelling space grew so did the value of the land. That is why many suburban courses laid out in the first twenty years of the twentieth century disappeared during the next decade. Speculators who had exploited the idea of a golf course as a selling point were succeeded by others who regarded 100 acres of golf ground as good building land wasted. In other cases land-owners who had leased space to clubs either succumbed to the temptation to profit by the demand for building land, or left their property to heirs who could not wait to turn the legacies to good account. So, in far too many cases, the green spot that had been a golf course turned almost overnight into regimented rows of houses.

London was particularly unfortunate in this respect for two reasons. It had the largest concentration of courses and was subject to the most intense housing development. What had been a 'great wen' in the eyes of William Cobbett was called a 'sprawl' by post-war conservationists, of whom Sir Patrick Abercrombie was foremost in demanding a halt to uncontrolled building. He was author of the Greater London Plan which included the idea of a Green Belt. But by the time the plan was published in 1944 the battle had been lost. Abercrombie proposed the transfer of 100,000 people to new towns well outside Greater London and a ban on building in between. This led to the Town and Country Planning Act of 1947 and the creation of a number of new towns in England, Scotland and Wales during the next decade. There was nothing new in town planning. The first of several Acts of Parliament relating to the problem was published in 1909 with the primary object of improving public health, although it also covered in theory the development and use of land. But the 1947 Act was the first to provide local authorities with powers to control land use, and came too late to prevent ribbon development on main roads, 'bungaloid growth' in dull suburbs, and the disappearance of many golf courses.

Raynes Park in Surrey, twelve miles from Charing Cross, provided a typical example of the effect of building development on golf. The course, laid out in 1893, was approached by walking across a field from a station which was then merely a halt. The hazards were hedges, brooks, great oaks and elms, and the inevitable artificial bunkers creating sandy holes in what had been a gentleman's park. The clubhouse was a modest pavilion considered adequate by local members who enjoyed their golf and the simple social pleasures connected with it. But after twenty years' enjoyment the golfers were made homeless. The land was sold to developers in 1923, the navvies and bricklayers moved in, and within a year or two nothing remained of the course save a few acres turned into playing fields and tennis courts. The clubhouse became the pavilion of a sports club, and some of the new roads were given names like Greenway, Linkway and Fairway, which reminded the displaced golfers of departed joys. Most of them went to the next parish, where the local council had resisted the speculative builder by deeming certain areas protected open spaces. Others lengthened their golfing journeys by joining clubs in the neighbouring countryside.

The story of Raynes Park Golf Club is that of many others in various parts of the country at that time. The dispossessed members carried on elsewhere, but a stretch of formerly open country had become a concrete sprawl, and that was irreversible. The landowners could not be criticized for profiting from the demand for land, nor the speculators for building. The fault lay in the absence of proper planning, which would have averted some of the worst effects of uncontrolled building, ensured the preservation of more green areas in the cities, and almost certainly saved some courses from extinction.

Nevertheless, the changes in the golfing map caused by development were almost invariably changes for the better. Many of the courses which disappeared had been pale imitations of the ideal, and although they satisfied the requirements of golfers who could rarely travel far afield for recreation, the loss in many cases was regarded not as a calamity but as an opportunity for finding something better. The march of progress, although involving the insensitive use of land, had also brought great improvements in transport in and out of cities so greatly extended. The development of the motor-car made it less important for the course to be within walking distance of the home. It could be ten or twenty miles away and still provide a full day's play without involving a night away from the family. Therefore the trend outwards from the city became more pronounced. The objective changed. Instead of local accessibility, the golfer looked for pleasant landscape, suitable subsoil and natural features in place of suburban dullness and artificiality. He also sought expert advice on using the latest methods of design and construction. So the commercially-minded developers of the 1920s did minimal damage to golf, because they pushed the players to better places and improved the golfing face of Britain.

Development outwards from city centres was characteristic of most populous places in Britain, but one of the most striking examples concerned the wedge of Greater London which, with its thin end on Marble Arch, extends northwards and westwards to embrace most of Middlesex and parts of Hertfordshire, Berkshire and Buckinghamshire. Before the Great War and for some time afterwards clubs were established at Wembley, Harrow, Acton, Neasden, Edgware and Hanger Hill, all in Middlesex and within twelve miles of central London. They all disappeared eventually, but not before the establishment of other clubs and courses further out. An important contribution to this development was made by the Metropolitan Railway Company in linking real estate enterprise with its primary task of transporting commuters between their working places in town and their residential quarters in the hilly parts of north Middlesex, Hertfordshire, and Buckinghamshire. Whereas most railways stemming from the centres of cities aimed at serving existing needs of the working population, and were extended as required, the Metropolitan was pushed out through comparatively open country and supplied the service which influences residential development. By providing longer and therefore more expensive journeys to pleasant country spots the controllers of 'Metroland' ensured selective building and avoided the sprawl then disfiguring London's inner suburbs. There was an emphasis on maintaining tone which, although smacking of snobbery, was a commercially sound policy carried out in many other parts of Britain. As a result the rural areas near our great cities and larger towns are dotted with places where the houses of prosperous business and professional men lie around or alongside golf courses, the two being interdependent.

Moortown, Sand Moor, the new course of the Moor Allerton Jewish club, and Alwoodley on the Earl of Harewood's estate form a group on the northern outskirts of Leeds. Around Birmingham are Copt Heath, Little Aston, Sandwell Park, Harborne and Edgbaston. Manchester's courses include those of the Mere Country Club and the Dunham Forest Club, both at Altrincham, which provide a striking contrast between the old idea and the new. Mere was laid out in an old-world estate round the lake which provides the name, and the existing mansion was converted for use as a clubhouse. Dunham Forest, on the other side of the main road to Manchester, was carved out of virgin land in 1960, and a modern clubhouse built after the mansion had been demolished.

Metroland's first golf courses were made at Chorley Wood on the Herts–Bucks border in 1890, and at Northwood, on the Herts–Middlesex border, in 1891. Chorley Wood was so exclusive a club that even twenty years after its formation the membership was limited to 150 and visitors were allowed to play only if accompanied by members. The Northwood club, being nearer London, was soon popular not only with the growing local population as Metroland developed, but also with London golfers who had lost their courses. The Ellesborough club was formed at Wendover in 1906, Harewood Downs at Chalfont St Giles in 1908, and Sandy Lodge near Northwood in 1910. Sandy Lodge had no direct association with the general residential policy of the Metropolitan Railway, although a station halt was constructed for the convenience of members. It was a geological accident, for the land used lay on one of the rare pockets of sand in that part of outer London, and was discovered by a golfer who had searched for a long time with that object in view. J. Francis Markes was a member of the Neasden club and, being bred a seaside golfer, sighed for something better than the London clay which made so many Middlesex courses hard-baked in summer and muddy in winter. Having been trained as a mining engineer in Australia he was a keen geologist, and his search for sand took him, one hot August day in 1908, to the Northwood district. Strolling along a footpath by a cornfield, he spotted some significant evidence at the mouth of a rabbit burrow. He investigated, and knew his search had ended. Having been referred by the tenant farmer to the landowner, Lord Ebury, who lived in Moor Park House on the other side of the railway, Markes obtained a lease on about 100 acres. With the help of Harry Vardon he laid out a course which reproduced, as nearly as possible, the characteristics of a seaside links, formed a club, and ruled it like a despot for the next forty years. He was the first Secretary and Lord Ebury the first President. Since Sandy Lodge Halt, when it was constructed, lay only a few yards from the clubhouse, the course was more accessible by railway than most others. That, and the sandy subsoil which made it playable at all times, ensured popularity with London golfers.

After the Great War an even more ambitious project started on the other side of the railway. In 1919 Lord Leverhulme, founder of Port Sunlight and therefore experienced in the development and management of estates, bought the historic Moor Park mansion and the park from Lord Ebury, made a golf course and sold the surrounding land in lots for the erection of exclusive houses. Moor Park now has two courses and is justly regarded as one of the most important inland golf centres. The residents exert rigid control over the area, barring public access to their private roads, and preserving the amenities by rules. But democracy and autocracy work together there as elsewhere. The public course owned by Rickmansworth Council marches with Moor Park's East Course and lies entirely within the boundaries of the 600-acre estate.

Moor Park was not the first development on such lines. In 1912 a Weybridge contractor, W. G. Tarrant, constructed St George's Hill, with fairways carved out of the woodland and heathland close to Brooklands motor track. Wentworth, scene of the Ryder Cup match, the World Cup and many other important events, was a business enterprise on the same lines—the purchase in 1924 of mansion and park, and the sale of building plots, all carefully controlled to maintain exclusiveness. But the great inland courses of England include many conceived by wealthy and influential men interested not in estate development but in providing pleasant places in which to play in privacy.

Nevertheless the exploitation of estates and the conservation of privacy in country areas could do nothing for the many thousands who have flocked to the game during the last forty years and are still increasing at an estimated rate of 50,000 a year. It has become very much more difficult for a few golfers to combine in starting a private course, and although several extravagant projects have been carried through in recent years, the main burden of providing facilities is falling more and more on the shoulders of municipalities and commercial undertakings. At one time local authorities were very shy of committing themselves to such enterprises, but it is now known that a public course properly administered can be profitable, and therefore be a community amenity at no cost to the ratepayer. The commercial exploitation of driving ranges and par-three courses helped, too, and the game in the 1970s was firmly orientated away from the old notions of privacy and exclusiveness. It had become once more a game of the people.

CHAPTER 18

Going public

Englishmen had been playing golf in England for nearly half a century before there was any move towards providing facilities for the public. The commons were open for general use, but in practice the golfers preserved for themselves the parts on which they played. When they began to enclose land to achieve real privacy the English game became still more removed from what it had been in Scotland for centuries. Scottish golfers started with public links and only gradually acquired private ones. Even today two of the most famous championship links, at Carnoustie and St Andrews, are publicly owned and open to all. Wherever one golfs in Scotland similar facilities are found. Nearly every burgh has its municipal course. The North Berwick links, on which socialites played in late Victorian and Edwardian days, is owned by the town. The Braid Hills course, one of the earliest and still one of the cheapest, has been used by generations of Edinburgh players, and many societies formed by craftsmen, professional men and commercial workers regarded 'The Braids' as their own. At Troon, on the west coast of Scotland there are, in addition to the Old Course owned by one of our most exclusive clubs, three municipal courses.

The case was far different in England and Wales, where golf was started by the upper classes and developed by business and professional men also able to pay for privacy and equally jealous of their rights. But it was inevitable that, as the lure of golf attracted more people from different walks of life, there should be a demand for facilities outside the private clubs. The artisan movement satisfied this need for some, but most artisan clubs were in rural districts with membership confined to local inhabitants. In any case the restrictions imposed on artisans were inconvenient and frustrating, particularly at week-ends when demand was greatest. The situation required courses available at all times to all comers, irrespective of age or sex, for moderate fees.

St Andrews was probably the last stronghold of the idea that because the links belonged to the people they could be used by everyone without payment. That privilege was enjoyed by all players on the Old Course, residents and visitors alike, until 1913. No doubt if golf had started in England much earlier than it did, some similar arrangement might have been allowed to continue, because the golfing commons were also used for public recreation and sports like football and cricket. But the gradual erosion of public rights to play golf was a natural result of the increasing cost of maintaining fairways and greens and the greater responsibilities of those in control. When golf was played from hole to hole along the coast and Mother Nature was the only green-keeper it was uncomplicated and inexpensive. As succeeding generations demanded more and more sophistication, and as man was forced to augment the efforts of nature, so it became necessary to get income for construction and upkeep. At first this was accomplished by golfers forming clubs, levying subscriptions and admitting non-members on payment of green fees. When the demand for golf necessitated the provision of public facilities, local authorities could either take over existing private courses and administer them for general use, or set aside land and money for the establishment of new ones.

Wimbledon Common in Surrey and Chingford and Hainault Forest in Essex provide examples of all three alternatives. Wimbledon Common is controlled by conservators who allow golf to be played but leave the London Scottish and Wimbledon Common Golf Clubs to collect subscriptions and green fees and share the cost of maintenance. Golf at Chingford was started in 1888 with the formation of the Royal Epping Forest club, and the course was taken over by the Corporation of London some twenty years later. (An artist's impression of the course at that time is shown in Plate 5.) The first example of a public course started for that purpose is Hainault Forest, laid out on a stretch of wooded country near Chigwell Row. The London County Council commissioned J. H. Taylor and his partner Fred Hawtree to design and construct a course which was opened in 1909. The fee was one shilling a round and a yearly season ticket cost two guineas. Despite the fact that Hainault was not then easily accessible by public transport the venture was successful from the start. This was not surprising, for the choice of location had been shrewd; the teeming working-class population of the East End and industrial Thames-side providing players most likely to benefit from cheap and unrestricted play. Hainault became so popular that after the Great War a second eighteen-hole course was made. Taylor also became convinced that conditions favoured a similar experiment on the western fringe of London. He assumed correctly that, golf having become a national game, the supply of facilities would never keep pace with the demand. His home course, Royal Mid-Surrey, was laid out in the Old Deer Park at Richmond, and he speculated on the chances of being able to use part of the huge expanse of Richmond Park on the other side of the town. With characteristic energy he pursued an object which, but for his enthusiasm and the co-operation of interested people with influence, might have remained unattainable.

Aware that the *Daily Mail* under Lord Northcliffe encouraged new ideas, Taylor initiated correspondence in that newspaper and received many offers of support, as well as some condemnations from people who regarded a golf course in a Royal park as akin to vandalism. He asked Lord Riddell to be chairman of a committee of leading golfers and, after several abortive talks with Earl Crawford and Balcarres, then HM Controller of Works, they obtained permission for the construction of an eighteen-hole course on 96 acres, on condition that no financial help would be expected from the Treasury. Far from helping with money, the Office of Works exacted £200 a year in rent, and the organizers faced the task of creating a viable undertaking from scratch and under the burden of overheads. It meant careful husbandry and a closer supervision of expenditure than would have been exercised by any government department or municipal authority. But any fears the pioneers might have had were groundless, for from the opening of the first Richmond Park Public Course by the Prince of Wales in June 1922, success was assured. Three years after this event another eighteen-hole course, constructed alongside the first, was opened by the Duke of York (afterwards George VI). It was typical of bureaucracy that the Office of Works, soon after the second course had been opened, and forgetting the refusal of financial help and the imposition of rent, invoked a clause in the agreement giving the government the right to take over the courses 'if thought desirable and expedient'. That is why the two Richmond Park courses are now managed by a superintendent taking his orders from Whitehall. But the thousands of golfers who play there, often queuing before dawn to get starting times at week-ends, owe their gratitude not to civil servants or politicians but to those who unselfishly pursued an aim with determination unquenched by official indifference and opposition.

Despite the success of the Richmond Park venture there were no further experiments for a long time in the south of England, although Birmingham showed considerable enterprise and that city now has seven public courses. So slow was the general development, due mainly to reluctance to spend ratepayers' money on what many ratepayers regarded as a rich man's luxury, that in 1946, a quarter of a century after Chingford had been acquired by the Corporation of London, only twelve clubs were affiliated to the National Association of Public Courses. Today more than seventy are in membership and many new municipal courses are under construction or in the planning stage. The reasons for this big spurt during the twenty-five years following the Second World War were chiefly economic. Prices of all goods and services had risen tremendously, and it was no longer possible for keen golfers to contribute a few hundred pounds and make a course. Costs were now quoted in thousands, suitable land had become scarce and therefore dear, and that also applied to labour. Taxation and the decreasing value of money took their toll of private means and discouraged indulgence in expensive projects. There were exceptions, but they were rare enough to emphasize the changed circumstances. Municipalities also had to contend with rising costs of labour and materials, but were much better placed for obtaining suitable land on cheaper terms than those available to private individuals, who were more likely to exploit any land they owned for building purposes. Local authorities also had management facilities for running golf courses. As a result the great majority of those built in England and Wales since 1946 have been started by municipalities, and the trend became still more marked following the formation in 1965 of the Golf Development Council. This body had as principal object cooperation with national and regional sports councils and with local authorities in stimulating the provision of playing facilities. The founder members were the Royal and Ancient Golf Club, the National Unions of England, Scotland, Wales and Ireland, the Ladies' Golf Union, the Professional Golfers' Association, Golf Foundation, the National Association of Public Golf Courses, and the Artisan Golfers' Association.

Active support came from the government-sponsored Sports Council under the chairmanship of Dr Roger Bannister, the first four-minute miler. One aim of the Sports Council is to encourage local authorities to develop centres catering for all games, with central pavilions providing changing-rooms and social facilities. By publishing facts and figures relating to the viability of golf courses, the GDC has done much good work in converting municipalities formerly sceptical. In November 1973 the Sports Council authorized grants of £247,625 towards the estimated cost of £1,617,500 for nine new municipal golf projects to be constructed in 1974–5. The grants were made on the recommendation of regional sports councils, with the local authorities concerned providing the balance. One course in Birmingham was planned as part of a complete outdoor recreation centre to cost in all £260,000. The other eight courses, with the estimated costs, were: Blyth (Northumberland), £125,000; Skelmersdale (Lancs.), £300,000; Widnes (Lancs.), £153,000; Bradford (Yorks.), £143,000; Grimsby (Lincs.), £80,000; Shrewsbury (Shrops.) £160,000; Welwyn Garden City (Herts.) £196,000; Hounslow (Middlesex), £200,500.

The Sports Council has called for 485 new courses to be built in Britain by 1981 to cope with the expected demand, and Dr Bannister has advocated putting the emphasis on municipal courses as in keeping with the current trend. In 1972 the first target announced by the Sports Council estimated a ratio of 8 public courses to 92 private. This was later revised to a ratio of 30 to 70 over the next few years.

Nevertheless, statistics for 1973 showed a trend in the opposite direction. During that year, in Britain, courses completed numbered 19 public and 19 private, but of 75 then under construction 48 were private and only 27 public. The comparative figures for 1972 had been: completed, 9 private, 12 public; under construction, 14 private, 26 public. But distinctions of this kind are of little importance beside the undoubted fact that considerable inroads had already been made into the Bannister backlog. The figures quoted, released by the Golf Development Council in February, 1974, showed that the target of 485 new courses by 1981 had been reduced by a third in a fifth of the time—174 in two years.

In many cases local authorities have gone into active discussion and co-operation with the GDC to achieve the best means of meeting the needs of golfers without expense to the ratepayers. Statistics prove the success of these efforts. From October 1971 to May 1973 ten new municipal courses were made and seventeen were under construction. In the same period four private courses were completed and eight under construction—clear evidence of the shift of emphasis. In many other cases, where shortage of land prevented full-scale schemes, municipalities and private firms have made driving ranges or complex golf centres to include range, putting green, par-three course and catering facilities. John Jacobs, a former Ryder Cup golfer who is managing-director of a company owning several golf centres, recently pointed out in an address to the Sports Council that these projects provide economical starting-points for beginners, enabling them to reach handicap standards before venturing on full-length courses to their own embarrassment and the frustration of more experienced users. As to viability, one of the biggest centres in the country, at Sandown Park racecourse at Esher, Surrey, showed an annual profit over two years of £30,000 despite losing each year, by theft, about 10,000 balls costing £1,500. An interesting comparison which I can recall from personal involvement at the time, concerns the action of the old Merton and Morden Council in Surrey, Socialist-controlled, doing away with a full-length course in Morden Park on the grounds that the Park belonged to the people, and ignoring the obvious fact that the golfers who played there were 'the people'. Twenty years later the same body, having been amalgamated with Wimbledon to become the Greater London Borough of Merton, built a par-three course in the same park which immediately proved more profitable than most of the community's other sporting facilities.

The public course of half a century ago lacked most of the amenities one would expect in a private club, and the social atmosphere was markedly different. But much has changed since then, in public taste and public life, and thousands of golfers are well content to pay their daily green fees or take out season tickets without wishing to seek membership of private clubs or feeling in any way at a disadvantage. Most of these courses now have adequate facilities, but the most important factor in their popularity is the considerable development of social and communal activities. Regular players soon form clubs and either provide their own quarters or are allotted rooms in the main buildings. It is rare that members of such clubs have any priority in the use of the course, although in some cases the authorities allow reservations of tee-times for competitions. But they enjoy many other advantages, including scope for holding competitions and so acquiring club handicaps. Most clubs are affiliated to the county unions concerned, and this enables all members to get proper handicaps, play in county events and be eligible for places in county teams. It is also helpful, for competitive and social reasons, to have matches against private clubs and therefore to play occasionally on private courses. Apart from other considerations, few private clubs are willing to accept raw beginners who, from lack of skill or ignorance of the rules and etiquette, will cause delays or damage on the course and inconvenience members. But if a novice has begun to play on a public course and can show his sponsors that he is reasonably efficient, his chances of private club membership are greatly increased.

Nevertheless the most up-to-date amenities and the most harmonious club atmosphere cannot compensate entirely for the gross overcrowding which public course golfers experience, particularly at week-ends. The private club can control use of the course at peak periods by limiting the number of members, charging heavy green fees for visitors, or banning visitors entirely unless introduced by members. No one can be barred from a public course if he has paid his money, and on Saturdays and Sundays the queues provide clear evidence of the difficulty. Lately there has been a healthy increase in the rate of providing extra facilities. It is probable that during the rest of the twentieth century the number of public courses, ranges and centres will have increased fivefold. Whether an increase of that kind will have kept pace with demand is another question.

CHAPTER 19

Caddies then and now

One of the minor results of changed conditions after the Second World War was a considerable reduction in the caddie population, due partly to the big increase in the financial demands of those who followed that casual but interesting occupation. The fees asked—at first £1 per round rising in a few years to £2 or more—were too high for the majority of players, and caddies concentrated their attentions on clubs of eminence and affluence, like Sunningdale, Berkshire, Walton Heath, Coombe Hill, Moor Allerton (Leeds), Potters Bar and Hartsbourne. At most clubs nowadays caddies are seen only on the occasion of important competitions, and the caddie-master, at one time almost as essential to club life as the professional and the steward, is a rarity.

When clubs were carried loose under-arm and the rough nature of the links demanded keen eyes to watch the fall of the ball, caddies were essential for those who could afford them, and those who could not carried their own clubs and laid them on the ground while playing a shot. The caddies of the feather-ball era could not have earned much, for even in the 1890s in England the price was rarely more than one shilling a round. When the Home Park club was started on Crown land at Kingston upon Thames in 1895, the caddies were paid sixpence for nine holes for 'first-class' men and fourpence for 'second-class' and boys, the club in each case taking a royalty of one halfpenny. These figures must be assessed in the light of other expenses at the time, for each of the club's founders guaranteed only £2, and the annual subscription was thirty shillings, the ladies paying half a guinea. The professional was paid £1 per week and had to look after the course in addition to his ordinary duties. There was no shortage of caddies eager to earn their sixpences and fourpences, and the halfpenny royalty added nearly £6 to the club's receipts in the first year.

Although costs rose with the years, it was possible even in the 1920s to engage a caddie for half a crown a round, of which two-pence or threepence went to the caddie-master as booking fee. Almost every club had a caddie-master, who kept the men and boys in order, allotted caddies in rotation, collected the fees from members and paid the caddies. The golfer would give his caddie six-pence for lunch money and a tip at the end of the day, having first made sure that the caddie had cleaned the iron clubs with emery paper and left them in good order at the caddie-master's hut. After the Second World War there was a wide difference of opinion between golfers who thought in terms of pre-war prices and caddies who valued their services in pounds instead of shillings. This led to much acrimonious correspondence in the golf magazines, but soon the ordinary club player became reconciled to the fact that he had to choose between shouldering his own bag or adding considerably to the cost of his golf. The answer to the problem came from the United States in the shape of a simple tubular frame on two wheels, on which the golfer could carry a bag of clubs, umbrella, water-proof clothing, and any liquid or solid refreshment required. The idea was elementary, the capital expenditure low, repairs and maintenance costs almost non-existent, and reliability virtually assured. Named caddie-cart at first and now universally known as a trolley, it cannot offer advice, clean clubs, replace divots or give the line for putting. But it is never late on parade, requires neither lunch money nor tip, and can be depended upon not to cough or sniff 'on the stroke' or make cynical comments on one's style to other caddies.

The first trolley to appear in Britain was imported by Lord Brabazon of Tara who, as Lt.-Col. J. T. C. Moore-Brabazon, had been a pioneer airman, a rider on the Cresta Run, and a golfer so born to the game that he transformed himself from tyro to scratch player in one summer. Never averse from experimenting with new ideas, he took his model to St Andrews for the R. and A. autumn meeting and solemnly pulled it round the Old Course while com-peting for the Medal, causing, as he recalled in his reminiscences, 'consternation among the caddies'. The human carriers must have reacted much as Allan Robertson and John Gourlay had to the appearance of the guttie ball. But whereas the guttie meant extinc-tion for the featherie, caddies remained in business, diminished in numbers but enjoying better and more prosperous conditions.

Meanwhile the first trolleys had spawned hundreds of different

PLATE I   An early engraving of the course at St Andrews with four
gentlemen players putting on the first green, having played across the
Swilcan Burn. No special clothes were worn and only a few clubs—here
carried underarm by their caddies—were used. The links was public
ground and pedestrians can be seen walking along Granny Clark's
Wynd towards the sea. The clubhouse is on the left and the buildings
on the right include the shops where Allan Robertson and Tom Morris
worked as ball makers.

PLATE 2   A putting match in progress beside the sea at Westward Ho!
ladies' golf club in 1873. Hartland Point may be seen in the background
and the marquee erected for the day and the horses and carriages in
attendance give the sense of a social occasion. The ladies are elaborately
dressed in their everyday clothes; only later were they to wear more
suitable golfing outfits.

HOUNSOM BYLES

PLATE 3 *Showing an ankle*

The manly swing and feminine style of this fashionably dressed lady golfer of the 1890s arouses the vicar's disapproval, the veteran's amusement and the young blood's grudging admiration.

A NATURAL ENQUIRY: "MUMMY, WHAT'S THAT MAN FOR?"

PLATE 4 *Date: 1906 Scene: a London suburb*

Even then a typically dressed golfer was the object of amazement, according to this *Punch* cartoon.

PLATE 5 *Chingford 1908*

The crowded first tee in front of the professional's hut shows just how popular golf became when public courses were first opened in England.

PLATE 6   Golf has always been a social game and one enjoyed by the highest echelons of society. But Churchill, pictured at Cannes in 1913 when he was First Lord of the Admiralty, does not seem to have accomplished a good shot. His everyday clothes do not, perhaps, suggest a very serious approach.

PLATE 7   This advertisement from 1920 makes the connection between a popular cigarette and a popular sport. Later, large tobacco firms became sponsors of golf, financing many tournaments. Note the golfers' 'uniforms'—the lady's long jacket with its high Tango-period waistline and mid-calf skirt, and the gentleman's orthodox plus-fours.

PLATE 8   The emancipated woman golfer, just before the Second
World War, exemplified by the Countess of Brecknock playing in a
charity match. Her macintosh trousers, parti-coloured shoes and free
swing suggest the dedicated amateur's commitment as she drives off
from the first tee.

PLATE 9   First off after lunch at St Andrews. The clubhouse, first real home of the Royal and Ancient, was built in 1853. It is now the background to many great events but also to the daily round of ordinary golfers. These players are sensibly dressed in the style of the 1950s. Trolleys were introduced in this country about 1950.

PLATE 10   Public enthusiasm gets the better of propriety in this charge to the 18th at St Andrews in the Walker Cup match, May 1971.

Vignettes

1   This sportsman of the 1860s is wearing typical golfing dress of suit and beret. The scene is Blackheath, in South London, where golf had to share the heath with passers-by.

2 Bunkers often took the form of
natural hazards. Here the caddy
holds the clubs underarm; golf
bags first appeared a decade later,
in the 1880s.

3 Casual onlookers and a passing
rider stop to watch a final putt on
one of the small greens.
Blackheath, 1869.

4   The fore-caddie, with his flag, was essential for showing the line of play. Here, on Blackheath in the 1860s, he stands on the edge of a large gravel pit with the green behind him.

5   Only one contestant seems to dissent from the popular acclaim as the Secretary finally announces the day's winner in this typical after-dinner scene of the 1870s.

models, all based on the simple idea of a framework on two wheels, costing a few pounds and virtually indestructible. Soon the out-buildings of most clubs had to include a storage shed, members pay-ing a small rent for trolley space. Ironically the now obsolescent caddie-master's hut was often converted to this use. Enterprising professionals laid in stocks of these machines for hire. The trolley had become ubiquitous, lacking only the human caddie's functions of holding the flagstick during putting, marking down the ball in flight, and giving advice and information. In the United States the hand type was succeeded by the sophisticated electric caddie-car, which could carry the player as well as his clubs and, in the case of larger models, both partners in a foursome with their equipment. This machine is rare in Britain, and when seen is almost always in use by golfers handicapped by age or disability. The idea has not been welcomed by British golfers, partly on the score of capital cost and battery-charging complications, but mainly because, unlike many rich Americans, they still regard the exercise of walking as an essential part of the game.

Those caddies who remain in business, now at £2 or more a round, are found at certain clubs at week-ends, in attendance on mid-week gatherings of societies, and in attachment to regular tournament professionals. Some of the best are travelling caddies, going to all the big events, frequently getting transport from the players employing them, and always certain of above average fees, good tips at the end of the meeting and, in the case of prize-money tournaments, a 'cut' of the winnings, often as much as five per cent. The modern travelling caddie has a much more pleasant and re-munerative life than did his predecessors, and basks in reflected glory if his 'man' does well. Some of them have regular arrange-ments with American and other overseas professionals visiting Britain, and become closely identified with the men they serve. Too closely in some cases, it can be inferred from a decision of the PGA in 1974 to impose a £50 fine on any professional whose caddie enters a clubhouse or locker-room during a PGA tournament, and a similar fine if his caddie fails to wear, throughout the round, the identification waistcoat provided by the sponsors. In some quarters this might be regarded as class discrimination, and if there were a caddies' union, often talked about but never yet formed, one would expect the militant shop-stewards to force industrial action. But such matters are of academic interest for the ordinary club golfer. For him the day of the human caddie has long since passed. The trolley, cheap, reliable, and uncomplaining, is as much part of the club golfer's equipment as his clubs and his shoes. But the status of the human caddies who remain has risen. Their life is far different from that of the Home Park caddies of 1896 and still further removed from the Northam Burrows in the 1870s, when a little fair-haired boy named John Henry Taylor caddied for sixpence a round with the knowledge that twopence of that would be docked if he lost a ball.

CHAPTER 20

Course and clubhouse

Golf club secretaries, green-keepers, professionals and stewards all have Associations to further and protect their interests and publish their own journals. That of the secretaries is given the apt title of *Course and Clubhouse*, for the modern secretary's work covers all indoor and outdoor activities and he controls the staffs concerned. Within living experience the functions and operational extent of the appointment have undergone significant changes, but there are even greater contrasts between the modern secretary and his predecessor of a hundred years ago. In those days courses required little attention, being mostly on natural links land. Clubhouses were modest buildings with rooms and furniture no more than adequate for simple tastes. Club servants were few in number and subservient in behaviour, and there were no complications about engaging and paying them. Therefore the secretary was usually a club member acting in an honorary capacity, sometimes doubling the post with that of treasurer. He had little to do and did not allow that to interfere with his golf.

The boom of the 1890s brought the first real change. Members of the new suburban clubs were mainly business and professional men with limited leisure and this fact, combined with more sophisticated ideas about clubhouse amenities, demanded staffing indoors and out on a scale not previously considered necessary. So many courses were being laid out in parkland and meadowland, often with unsuitable subsoils, that proper maintenance required more than an occasional run-over with the mower or cropping by sheep. Lush, fast-growing grass, artificial bunkers with imported sand, deciduous trees with their seasonal leaf-fall, all required frequent attention; and increased wear and tear as memberships grew involved clubs in considerable expenditure on labour and materials, as well as creating the need for day-to-day supervision of staff.

The day of the honorary secretary, turning up on Saturdays to receive competition entries and then dashing out to compete on his own account, calling committee meetings to suit his own arrangements, and paying wages in intervals between rounds, was passing. It became necessary to appoint full-time paid secretaries who were really managers, since they were responsible to the members for seeing that the work in and out of the clubhouse was carried on efficiently and economically. Nevertheless until the Great War the secretarial post, if not a sinecure, usually provided a pleasant existence. There was time for a game on mid-week afternoons after dealing with the mail and disposing of work-discussions with steward and green-keeper. With little interruption from members save at week-ends, and with an obsequious staff at his command, the average secretary in those days was comfortably situated. He was usually in retirement from Service or civil life, with a pension which enabled him to accept a comparatively modest salary for doing work which, interspersed as it was with occasional rounds of golf and pleasant social interludes, could not be termed onerous. The average salary sixty years ago was about £200, supplemented in some cases by free lunches and an entertainment allowance, and not infrequently by living quarters.

Post-war conditions changed the picture dramatically. War-time regulations, including rationing, continued for a long time afterwards and the secretary became involved in restrictions, form-filling and other paper work which was to grow in extent and complexity over the next half-century. Gradually the regular afternoon round dwindled to a few holes snatched when opportunity offered. More and more members took to playing golf in mid-week. It was necessary to cater for visiting societies. The ladies became independent spirits and made demands on the secretary's time and patience. Green-keepers, by now mostly qualified men, tended to take control of their departments. Stewards—and their wives—also had independent ideas and the will to express them. Members grew more exacting and critical. Captains and treasurers developed enquiring minds. The old type of secretary, whose main qualification was a willingness to live on his pension and a moderate salary, was succeeded by one well able by experience to handle a mass of paper-work and control staff who were themselves better qualified than their predecessors.

Most of these changes stemmed from the fact that maintenance and administration had become much more costly and the members expected the club to be self-supporting. Most of the earliest clubs in England were started by well-to-do upper class golfers who could be relied upon to contribute without demur towards any special expenditure not covered by the modest subscriptions. Today most golf clubs must meet costs by the receipts from subscriptions, bar and catering profits, and income from indoor social activities and games, including primarily the ubiquitous 'one-armed bandit'. That, simply, is the reason for the frequent increases in subscriptions made since the Second World War.

The modern secretary is trained for the job. He is still often a retired officer, bank manager or civil servant, but in addition to being experienced in book-keeping, correspondence and administration, he must have a working knowledge of green-keeping and understand the complexities of catering and bar operation. He has the responsibility of buying supplies and checking stocks for both clubhouse and course. And the introduction of VAT in 1973 merely added to the complexities of the job. No wonder the secretary of today spends most of his time in his office and goes on to the course mainly to inspect the work of the green-keeping staff.

Green-keepers and stewards are also qualified men dedicated to busy lives. The former must have a sound knowledge of turf maintenance and pest control and the use of many modern chemicals. He has charge of expensive machinery and controls men whose labour must be used economically. He acquires his knowledge and keeps up to date with new ideas by attending lectures and practical demonstrations, and on his skill depends the health of the course and therefore the satisfaction of the members. The steward must have the art of pleasing members and controlling staff, and be prepared to work long or at least awkward hours. It is usual for a man and his wife to work as steward and stewardess, living on the premises. Many clubs undertake evening catering for parties, which means engaging extra staff and keeping large and varied stocks of wines and spirits. The modern clubhouse is full of activity seven days a week, and so much depends on green-keeper and steward that each in his own sphere is an important person. Whereas the green-keeper sixty years ago was paid little more than the average wage of a farm worker, he must now be tempted and retained by a realistic salary and fringe benefits. A head green-keeper can expect from £1,500 to £2,000 a year with rent and rate-free accommodation. A steward and his wife would receive together £2,000 a year or more with a free flat in the clubhouse and full board.

When the mower was often the only important bit of machinery in the green-keeper's hut, the job was scarcely more complicated than that of a gardener, and the individual holding it would be expected to carry out instructions rather than initiate operations. Similarly the steward has been transformed from a man in a white coat running a bar at week-ends into an expert in sophisticated catering responsible for a variety of services. The general effect has been to bring the green-keeper and steward more on a social level with the people employing them, and the usually harmonious relations between them and the members make a distinct contrast with the remote master-and-man relationship in the early days of English club golf.

Most of the Scottish clubs cling to the old idea of an honorary secretary who merely handles ordinary club affairs and has only a superficial control over administration. All the operations inside the clubhouse are directed by a manager, called a club-master, who is a combination of steward and English-type secretary, while the green-keeper rules his own kingdom outside. Whatever the arrangements, golf club administration is now so specialized that efficiency above and below stairs, inside and out, is important, but not more important than the preservation of harmonious relations all round. It follows that few secretaries can emulate the men who were known in their day as martinets, ruling their domains and everyone in them—including the members—with iron hands. Harold Janion of Hoylake, F. P. Lemarchand of Sunningdale, J. R. Montgomerie of Royal Mid-Surrey, and H. Ryder Richardson of Deal, are names which might still bring a shiver of apprehension into the hearts of golfers who flourished fifty years ago. They and others like them were autocratic and, so far from submitting problems to their committees, took decisions on their own without fear of being overruled.

A story told of Montgomerie will illustrate the point. He was walking the corridor at Royal Mid-Surrey and found a very new and very young member searching among the magazines on a table.

'Can I help you?' he asked amiably.

'I'm looking for the suggestion book,' stammered the youngster.

Montgomerie's brow clouded as he drew himself to his full height.

'Young man,' he exclaimed, touching his chest with forefinger, 'in this club *I* am the suggestion book.'

There have been changes, too, in the character and status of the golf club captain. In the earliest days the office was filled automatically by the winner of the annual medal competition. John Rattray, the Edinburgh surgeon, was the first 'Captain of the Goff' in 1744 because he won the first competition for the silver club at Leith. In that position he handled subscriptions, competition fees and other dues, and settled all disputes arising during play. He also presided at the dinners after golf. When the number of golfers concerned was small it was natural to regard the best player as leader. But in large and heterogeneous communities of sportsmen, particularly those playing team games like cricket and football, the captain is usually chosen less for his superiority in performance than for his qualities as leader and tactician, his popularity and his social bearing. In some of these respects golf is a less demanding game, and for a long time, in some cases even down to the present century, clubs adhered to the practice of making the captaincy a competitive office. The principle was adopted when competitions started at St Andrews, and the winner of the silver club automatically became captain. But around the beginning of the nineteenth century this arbitrary system was changed to an elective captaincy, the election at St Andrews being by a committee of past captains, as it is to this day. Yet, in keeping with the Briton's traditional conservatism, the idea that the winner of the silver club must be captain is perpetuated in a ceremony which takes place at St Andrews at the autumn meeting each year—the captain 'driving into office'. At eight o'clock on medal day the captain-elect hits a ball from the first tee of the Old Course while an ancient cannon is fired to inform all St Andrews that he has done so. The inductant goes through the ritual of presenting a sovereign or some equivalent to the caddie retrieving the ball, and disappears, to return later and compete with all the other members for the Royal Medal and the Gold Medal. In effect the shot he played in ceremony represented the first stroke in the competition for the silver club. Since no other member came forward to contend for the prize, the captain-elect automatically became captain, notwithstanding the fact that his election had been announced six months earlier at the spring meeting.

During the years of the competitive system it must have produced more than one captain who was not wholly acceptable, since prowess on the links is not necessarily accompanied by likeable attributes. Nevertheless it persisted in other quarters long after it had been abandoned at St Andrews, with some curious results. For example, Horace Hutchinson found himself in the captain's chair of the Royal North Devon club, at the age of sixteen, because he had won the scratch gold medal. Evidently this was a shock for the senior members, because the club rules were immediately changed to provide for formal election.

Administration of the modern club demands decentralization o tasks and responsibilities. There are green committees, house committees, finance committees, all composed of members of the general committee, and the captain, by this delegation of authority, is free to attend to the social side and overall scrutiny of the club's activities. Many clubs today are constituted as limited companies, with members serving as directors, in which case the functions of the captain are limited almost entirely to competitive and social affairs.

Of course golf club life is now far different from the days when the players were all men and the internal administration was simple. Instead of one medal day a year and dinners in masculine exclusiveness after matches, the modern club has an extensive fixture list with regular monthly and bi-monthly competitions, running knock-out events, and social gatherings like dances and dinners, in all of which the ladies, sometimes in their own clubs but often in company with the men, play a full part. The captain of the 1970s must be all things to all men—and all women—but a low handicap is not one of the essential qualifications.

CHAPTER 21

Golf in company

Another product of the golf boom of the
1890s was the modern Golfing Society founded by golfers, often
drawn from many different clubs, who had mutual interests or
represented particular schools, colleges and professions. The earliest
associations of golfers at Leith, St Andrews and Brunts Field were
known as societies. The Royal and Ancient Golf Club of St
Andrews started as the Society of St Andrews Golfers, and to this
day we have the ancient Burgess Society of Bruntsfield existing as
the Royal Burgess Golfing Society at Barnton. But these and other
eighteenth-century bodies, composed of local golfers, were clubs in
the modern sense. The societies starting in the 1890s drew members
from many localities, and club affiliations had no significance. In
Scotland during the latter part of the nineteenth century, players
using the many public courses formed numerous societies and held
their competitions without having any priority in the use of the
links. At one time no fewer than 126 'clubs' were listed for the
Edinburgh area alone, but only seventeen were attached to or
owned courses. The majority were societies, and covered a wide
field of human activities and interests. The staffs of banks, insurance companies and other commercial firms had their own circles.
So did several churches, the local schools and colleges, newspapers,
and employees of public service undertakings. Doctors, dentists and
lawyers formed themselves into societies. The longest title was The
British Order of Ancient Free Gardeners' Friendly Society Golf
Club; and the oddest Ye Monks of Ye Braids Golf Club. Although
many of these have disappeared others have been formed and the
Golfers' Handbook today lists more than 500 in Britain, mostly based
in London.

Almost any reason seems to be sufficient for the formation of a society, and the object is often no more serious than the desire for a good time together, with golf almost a secondary consideration. But mainly the impulse comes from the tendency for men and women of similar habits, occupations and interests to share occasionally the pleasures of golf in congenial and familiar company. Many societies have been formed for charitable purposes, and others for organizing tours or supporting particular projects. The most celebrated of the early ones is the Oxford and Cambridge Golfing Society, founded in 1898. The Oxford v. Cambridge match had been running for twenty years and several of those who took part in the early contests, including Horace Hutchinson and W. T. Linskill, were among the founder members, with the Rt Hon. Arthur James Balfour, then Leader of the House in Lord Salisbury's government, as President. Mr Balfour left Cambridge some years before the start of University golf, but he had played the game from boyhood and pursued it with keenness throughout his political career. The society's first secretary, a schoolmaster named Arthur Croome who later was golf correspondent for the *Morning Post*, was another member who never played for his university, but most of the founders were old blues, and in their day a golfer had to be very good, scratch or not much worse, to get a place in his 'varsity team. So when the young society organized a tour of the United States in 1903 they were representative of British amateur golf, and when international matches were started twenty years later the British teams against the United States were at least 50 per cent Oxbridge in colour. In those days a good games player could remain up at either university and concentrate more on getting a blue than on studying for a degree. Now the situation is different. The intake of Oxford and Cambridge represents a much wider spectrum of British life; the emphasis is on study rather than sport, and the quality of university golf teams has suffered accordingly.

Golfers of many other universities are similarly organized, and the old boys of public schools hold periodical meetings and take part in inter-school matches and tournaments. The most important of these is for the Halford-Hewitt Cup, competed for each Eastertide by former pupils of leading schools and involving more than 600 players, each team consisting of ten men playing foursomes throughout. During that week-end at Sandwich and Deal the corporate spirit is seen at its best. Each society has a regular booking at one particular hotel, and wooden shields bearing the school crests are placed on appropriate tables at meal-times. Apart from its convivial side, often in evidence, the tournament greatly increases the enthusiasm for golf among pupils at the various schools, and there is now another competition, for the Grafton-Morrish Cup, in which teams of existing scholars compete.

Almost every trade and organization is represented among the hundreds of societies. The Seniors' GS, for players over fifty-five, has periodical battles with similar bodies in Canada and the United States. There is a society for left-handed players, another for one-armed golfers. The theatrical and variety artists have their separate societies. As they work mainly in the evening the Stage and Vaudeville Society members, together with taxi-drivers, policemen, musicians and film actors, play most of their golf on mid-week mornings and some have arrangements with certain clubs to provide playing facilities at inclusive annual fees.

Although the emphasis in most society golf is on fraternal and communal interests some bodies have considerable influence. The Golf Society of Great Britain, for example, has an arrangement with twenty clubs in different parts of the country, where all GSGB members can play free of charge. The Lucifer GS, formed to play matches against other institutions, organizes a big annual competition in which golfers from the Commonwealth countries compete. The Hazards GS, which has a limit of 125 active members admitted only by invitation, is responsible for the annual boys' competition for the Carris Trophy, which has given many fine golfers their first competitive successes.

Society golf, with so many objectives ranging from the enjoyment of pure fun to the promotion of serious projects, makes two important contributions to the game in Britain. It provides many players with facilities which they would not otherwise have, and gives welcome revenue to the clubs visited.

CHAPTER 22

Golf as news

With millions playing the world over and with newspapers, radio and television giving much space and time for reporting big competitions and publicizing stars, the image of golf is universally familiar. But this is a latter-day situation. A hundred years ago only those who played understood the game—it was a closed book for the general public. In 1888, when the first American club was established, the pioneers were prosecuted for playing on Sundays, and the case collapsed because 'golf' was not in the legal vocabulary. But during the next few years circumstances changed, and the formation of the USGA in 1894 led to a broadening of public interest. Meanwhile, in Britain, the demand for information and guidance about golf was already being met by the publication of journals and books to supply a growing market. It would seem that the spread of golf beyond Scotland was essential to the development of literature, for very little had been published prior to the middle of the nineteenth century. One of the earliest printed references, apart from official documents, was a poem in a book of verses published in Perth in 1638. A poem about golf on Glasgow Green, issued in 1721, was followed in 1743 by the celebrated verses of Thomas Mathison, produced in Edinburgh by J. Cochran. This work, describing many famous characters on Leith links who were soon to form the Honourable Company, was republished in 1763 and again in 1795.

The first publication outside Scotland mentioning golf was an edition of *Hoyle's Games Improved*, published in London in 1808, price six shillings and including a chapter on 'The Game of Goff or Golf'. During the next fifty years several books referring to the game came from Scottish presses, but the subject-matter was of a discursive character. The Rev. C. A. Lyon's *History of St Andrews*

(Edinburgh, 1843) included a chapter on the Royal and Ancient Club; and John Kay's *Edinburgh Portraits* five years earlier had some references to golfing personalities in the capital. A significant occurrence around that time was the re-issue of George Fullerton Carnegie's *Golfiana*. This collection of pieces had appeared in 1833 for private circulation, dedicated to members of the North Berwick club. The edition of 1842 was offered to the public at five shillings and dedicated 'to members of all golf clubs'.

By that time several clubs had printed their own rules, and the volume containing those of the Thistle Club of St Andrews, produced in 1824, also included a history of golf. The rules of the Manchester (now Old Manchester) club were printed in 1828 by J. Aston, of Manchester, which suggested that this body, founded in 1818, had quickly established a local importance. Although several books already mentioned had references to methods of play, the nineteenth century was more than half over before the first 'how to play' book appeared for general circulation. In 1856 a *Manual of British Rural Sports* (Routledge, London) had a section devoted to golf; and in the following year the *Golfers' Manual*, by a 'Keen Hand' was produced by Whitehead and Orr of Cupar, near St Andrews. It was sub-titled *An Historical and Descriptive Account of the National Game of Scotland*, and the author, H. B. Farnie, covered all aspects of his subject—the history, comparisons between feather-ball and guttie-ball eras; classification of clubs, detailed playing instructions, hints on tactics and philosophic reflections. It was the first complete survey of the game, and remained unchallenged for years.

In 1866 W. and R. Chambers of Edinburgh produced one of their sixpenny handbooks dealing with gymnastics, curling and golf—not such strange bedfellows, since curling is a Scottish game and golfers even then no doubt resorted to something like gymnastics in their efforts to coax the ball into the hole. In the following year the publication in Ayr of the *Golfers' Yearbook*, price one shilling, was a symptom of growing interest not unconnected with the Open Championship, then exclusively played on the Prestwick links.

The big event of 1875 was the publication of *Golf: a Royal and Ancient Game* by the Edinburgh publisher Robert Clark. It was a symposium of all that had gone before, together with interesting details of the early days of the oldest clubs, and has been a useful work of reference ever since. In the same year Joseph Strutt's *Sports*

and Pastimes of the People of England was published in London, and
although 'England' in this context probably meant Britain, the
period was in fact one of growth in the number of English players.
Even more significant was the inclusion of an article on golf in the
Encyclopædia Britannica (9th edition) which came out in 1879. The
remaining twenty years of the century saw a steady increase in the
number and variety of publications, beginning with the *Golfers'
Handbook*, compiled by Robert Forgan of the St Andrews club-
making family, and published by J. and G. Innes of Cupar. Charles
E. Chambers, of the Edinburgh publishing house, issued *Golfing—A
Handbook of the Royal and Ancient Game*, in 1887 and in the same year
appeared *The Art of Golf*, by Sir Walter G. Simpson, Bart, with
'instantaneous photographs' by A. F. MacFie, who two years
earlier had won the first Amateur Championship. The rules did
not then preclude amateurs from writing instructional material,
and the age of ghosts for professionals had not dawned. In any case
there were many amateurs of championship rank much more capable than the leading professionals of analysing techniques and,
with superior education, better able to express themselves with the
pen. They included W. T. Linskill, a co-founder of Cambridge
University Golf Club, who in 1889 contributed to the All-England
series published by G. Bell in London; and Horace Hutchinson,
Oxford Blue and editor of the *Golf* volume in the Badminton
Library, issued in 1890 by Longmans, Green of London. That year
also saw the appearance of the first periodical, called *Golf: a Weekly
Record of the Royal and Ancient Game*. This appeared regularly until
June 1899, when it was absorbed by a new weekly, the present *Golf
Illustrated*, now published by Harmsworth Press.

A rival magazine, the *Golfer*, began as a penny weekly in 1895, in
Edinburgh, was converted to a threepenny monthly in 1898 and
disappeared in 1900. A more successful publication, which lasted
for more than fifty years before being absorbed in the modern
weekly *Golf International*, was *Golfing*. It started as a penny weekly in
1897 with the title *Golfing and Cycling*, but the second subject was
dropped in 1899 and the publication became a monthly. The next
periodical was the *Irish Golfer*, published in Dublin as a penny
weekly, which became a fortnightly during the winter. Very little
news-worthy golf was played in winter and few if any reports came
from overseas, so that golf, from the point of view of both editors
and advertisers, was a summer game. But already interest was being
created abroad, and the closing years of the century were notable

for several productions in the United States, beginning in 1895 with *Golf*, by James White, published in Boston, Massachussetts, and *Golf in America*, 'a practical manual', by James P. Lee, published by Dodd Mead & Co. of New York. This, and the *American Cricket Annual and Golf Guide* of 1896, followed closely on the formation of the United States Golf Association. In 1897 H. J. Whigham, member of a leading West of Scotland golf family and then resident in America, published *How to Play Golf*. The title was uncompromising; it was golf instruction written by an amateur. And it came out in the very year that the Rules of Golf Committee was formed at St Andrews, and started to move towards more rigid definitions of amateurism.

Back in Britain, 1896 saw the first book by a professional—the *Game of Golf* by William Park, Jnr, a 277-page volume issued by Longmans, Green (London) at 7/6d. This was possibly an unaided production by the author who was, as already pointed out, a shrewd and capable business man, possessing up-to-date views and able to express them. In the following year appeared what seems to have been the first 'ghosted' book *Golf*, by J. McBain and W. Fernie, published by Dean (London). McBain was a well-known west of Scotland amateur player and administrator, and Willie Fernie, winner of the Open in 1883, was professional at Troon.

With the dawn of the twentieth century and the arrival of the rubber-core ball, the flow of books and publications began to rise towards the present-day flood. By this time, too, newspapers were taking more than a passing interest in golf and the performances of the leading players. There is today immense coverage of the Open Championship by newspapers, radio and television, but the early years of that event passed almost unnoticed by the Press outside Scotland. The *Ayr Advertiser* devoted most space to the day's play at Prestwick in 1860, and this was not surprising since there was considerable local interest. But that event and several subsequent ones were practically ignored outside Scotland. The first Open to be reported by *The Times* was that of 1876 at St Andrews, and the short mention was given second place to the account of the autumn meeting of the R. and A., in the same week. The R. and A. meeting was held first, and after some two hundred members had contested their various medals for three days, the professionals had their turn. In those days amateurs were the important people in golf and this first *Times* report, which began: 'The Autumn meeting of the Royal and Ancient Golf Club was appropriately brought to a close on

Saturday by the annual competition for the Championship', made
that crystal clear.

The amateur victories of John Ball in 1890 and Harold Hilton
in 1892 helped to establish the Open as worthy of more attention,
and the performances of J. H. Taylor, Harry Vardon and James
Braid in subsequent years added still more to its prestige. By that
time newspapers all over Britain were carrying reports of the principal events, and when the *News of the World* started the knock-out
tournament in 1903, first of a series which lasted more than fifty
years and is still being promoted by other sponsors as the PGA
match-play championship, the professional game began to move
towards its present-day importance. A prize-money tournament
was not new, but a newspaper sponsorship was, and most of the big
professional competitions held during the next thirty years were
started by periodicals. Nowadays we are accustomed to the names
of commercial sponsors. Newspapers have gone out of the running,
because the prize money demanded is considerable, and worth
while only for large firms dealing in commodities who find golf and
other sports attractive means of advertising their products. Until
after the Great War the *News of the World* remained alone in the
field of newspaper sponsorship, apart from some provincial journals
giving modest support to local events; but in 1919 the *Daily Mail*
promoted a £500 tournament, and later began a series of annual
promotions. During the same period big tournaments were staged
by the *Glasgow Herald*, the *Yorkshire Evening News*; and among London papers, the *Daily News* and the *Star*. Today no newspaper is
concerned in big golf promotion. Of the fourteen British tournaments decided in 1973, five were backed by tobacco firms, three by
the drink trade, three by clothing manufacturers, two by golf ball
makers, and one by a concern having no connection with golf. (But
the connections between a popular sport and a popular commodity
have often been stressed, as the advertisement from the 1920s, reproduced in Plate 7, shows.)

Nevertheless, newspaper interest in golf had grown with the
years. All national newspapers, and many of the principal provincial journals, have accredited golf correspondents, while nearly
every local newspaper has someone on the staff who covers events
of district interest. There are two monthly magazines and two
weeklies with national circulations, and books in many hundreds
have come from the presses in Britain and America during the last
fifty years. These are in three main categories—purely instruc-

tional, purely biographical, and a mixture of the two. The biggest reader demand is for instructional articles and books, because the keen club golfer is for ever searching for the cure of all his ills and the secret of success.

The importance of the newspapers is fully appreciated by sponsors and promoters, including the clubs on whose courses the big events are played, but this was not always the case. Before the Great War only the quality newspapers employed golf correspondents, the most celebrated being Bernard Darwin, a grandson of Charles Darwin, who wrote for *The Times* anonymously as 'Our Golf Correspondent'. His contemporary on the *Morning Post* was Arthur Croome, first secretary of the Oxford and Cambridge Golfing Society. They, and a few others, including Sir Guy Campbell, an occasional contributor to *The Times*, had the entrée to golf clubs during the Amateur and Open Championships, but most of the journalists attending those events shared with the professionals the frustration and frequent embarrassment of being barred. It was a considerable advance for golf journalists when, on the occasion of an amateur championship at St Andrews, they were allowed to enter the R. and A. clubhouse on payment of 25s. for the week, provided they had been vouched for by Bernard Darwin. This concession did not satisfy them, and in 1938, to establish a campaigning platform for better treatment for all at every championship club, they formed the Association of Golf Writers and elected as President—Bernard Darwin. There were about twenty founder members but today there are more than eighty, including representatives of newspapers and news agencies, radio and TV commentators and some foreign writers.

The founders did not immediately achieve all their aims, but increasing co-operation from promoters and a gradual retreat by championship clubs from their conservative attitudes combined to give the golf Press complete enjoyment of all facilities at major events. The golf writer of today, whether he represents a national newspaper or an obscure local journal, is unhampered and welcomed. He is courted by sponsors, and his comfort and working conditions are high on the list of planning essentials. The most powerful factor in these changes was the commercialization of golf. Gate money was not charged at championships until 1926. Before then, and for a long time afterwards, host clubs were not greatly concerned about the welfare of spectators or even, in some cases, the competitors. The average journalist was regarded as a nuisance, or at best a necessary evil. He was provided with a tent in which to work, but was not expected to enter the clubhouse, unless, like Darwin, Croome and a few others, he belonged to the right class. But once the championships began to produce revenue, the importance of the Press as a publicizing medium grew, and the transformation was completed by the developments of tournaments sponsored by commercial firms only too anxious to ensure newspaper coverage and the good will of the writers.

Long before those days arrived, radio had become an important source of information. Coverage of golf began in the late 1920s with the BBC broadcasting reports of the championships, but this was at first immature and haphazard. The early radio reporters were not 'live' commentators, but delivered short reports at the end of the day, often as part of news bulletins. The ubiquitous Bernard Darwin was one of the first to undertake this work and in his reminiscences (*Golf Between Two Wars*, Chatto & Windus, 1944), he relates one of his early experiences. In 1930 Bobby Jones won the Open at Hoylake as part of his grand slam—the winning of the Open and Amateur Championships of Great Britain and the United States in one season. If Macdonald Smith, a Scot from America, could get a birdie three at each of the last two holes he could tie with Jones, so Darwin went out to meet him. He wrote (page 72):

> I could not go far because I had to broadcast and the time was getting hideously short. I saw him [Macdonald Smith] play the Royal [the 17th hole]—I was to broadcast from a house not far off—and his putt for a three did not go in. Two to tie and surely that was impossible, but . . . I waited till his second had pitched on the green and had palpably not holed out. Then I ran and ran and arrived just in time to announce to a breathless world that Bobby had won again.

The hyperbolic 'breathless world' apart, those words paint a picture of radio coverage of a very *ad hoc* kind, even to using a private telephone in someone's house. But at that time a special telephone was a rarity in the Press tent, and usually installed only by news agencies. *The Times* and most other morning newspapers relied on Press telegrams which were despatched at a special cheap rate—eighty words for a shilling. Even the evening paper reporters, for whom speed was everything, used Press telegrams too—at sixty words a shilling—and the lunch-time editions, which now carry a complete story of the morning play, would contain information only about the first few holes of the day. Anyone wanting to telephone and having no special installation would rely on obtaining permission—rarely refused—to use an instrument in a private house.

For years radio coverage of big golf was restricted to reports telephoned at the end of the day's play, and these naturally lacked the immediacy which provides drama. In 1946, when the Open Championship was revived at St Andrews, I was among those who helped Stewart McPherson to carry out the first running commentary on golf. He sat on the verandah of the R. and A. clubhouse with a microphone and relied on progress reports from the course via a field telephone system operated by Army volunteers, and occasional comments from collaborators. In 1951 the BBC went a stage further by stationing observers at different points on the Royal Portrush links, and so achieving the first live commentary on 'golf as it happens'. Radio coverage today requires a broadcasting van connected by landline to the BBC and, in addition to commentators, a local producer and technicians.

Early TV coverage, which started in the 1950s, was limited to edited film of the day's events with a dubbed commentary, usually included in a news bulletin. But as public interest grew much more was needed, and so began the march to the present elaborate organization which costs thousands of pounds for each event and employs hundreds of people. For the 1973 Open Championship at Troon the BBC had cameras at thirteen different places on the links, so that only the ninth and tenth holes were out of view. With five commentators and a quick-thinking production team switching from camera to camera, nothing vital was missed during the four days, and the invaluable technique of video play-back added emphasis to the exciting moments, including the unforgettable slow motion of Gene Sarazen's hole-in-one at the 8th. Another advantage of slow motion was the opportunity it provided for experts in the commentary box to analyse styles and methods of the players. Many other sports besides golf are televised extensively by the BBC and the commercial channels, but golf, because it is spread over a large area, differing in character from course to course, has special problems which can only be overcome by careful and expensive preparations. The cost seems to be worth while, because in 1973 no fewer than ten of the main British events were televised on one channel or another.

The importance of television for publicizing the sponsoring firms cannot be exaggerated, and in every way the modern prize-money tournaments are worlds removed from those of the inter-war years. A century ago the modest prizes for the few small events were subscribed for by members of a club who wanted to see the leading players in action. The organization was minimal and often non-existent. So was newspaper interest, and the small galleries were composed entirely of golfers. Today the important tourna-ments are followed physically by thousands (see Plate 10), and vicariously by millions using radio and television. Many of the latter are not players at the start, but learn the technique and finer points of the game by looking and listening. In many cases interest turns to active participation. But as with cricket, equestrianism, athletics, swimming, racing and other sports in the public eye, the radio and television audiences are composed mainly of non-parti-cipants. They are being entertained, and the value of sport in the entertainment field has never been higher than it is today. Nor has the image of golf been more clearly portrayed.

CHAPTER 23

Royalty on the links

Golf is most appropriately known as the Royal and Ancient Game because it is centuries old, and there have been few periods in its history without the patronage or participation of kings and princes. The Stuart monarchs of Scotland played and the last of them, James VI, introduced golf to England on his accession as James I of the United Kingdom. Charles I was also addicted, for he was playing in a match on Leith links in 1641 when a messenger brought news of the rebellion in Ireland. Four years later, while imprisoned by the Scottish army at Newcastle, Charles was allowed to go beyond the castle walls to play golf 'in the Shield fields'—an area at the mouth of the Tyne which in those days might well have been excellent golfing country. James II, when Duke of York and living in Edinburgh as Commissioner for his brother Charles II, also played at Leith in the comparatively care-free days before his troubled years on the throne. After the overthrow of the Stuart dynasty, many years passed without any recorded royal interest in golf, neither by William III nor by the early Hanoverians, although George IV probably became acquainted with it during his regency. Reawakening royal involvement was put into concrete terms by William IV, one of whose titles was the Duke of St Andrews. In 1834 he consented to become patron of the St Andrews Society, and approved the change of title to 'The Royal and Ancient Golf Club of St Andrews'.

Three years later J. Murray Belshes, then captain of the R. and A., received this letter from Major General Sir Henry Wheatley at St James's Palace:

> Sir, I have the honour to transmit, by the King's command, a
> Gold Medal, with green ribband [*sic*], which His Majesty desires
> you will present in his name to the Royal and Ancient Golf Club

of St Andrews, and which His Majesty wishes should be challenged and played for annually by that Society.

A few weeks afterwards the king died. His widow Queen Adelaide, who became Queen Dowager on the accession of her niece Victoria, but was still Duchess of St Andrews, consented to become Patroness of the Club, and in 1838 presented a medal with the request that it should be worn by the captain on all public occasions. It was named the Royal Adelaide Medal and the queen's wishes have ever since been carried out by successive captains.

For some years afterwards there was no noticeable royal interest, for a queen was on the throne and her consort was no lover of sport. But Victoria's eldest son, Edward Prince of Wales, became acquainted with golf in his youth and remained involved with it throughout his life. While in his teens he lived for a time in Edinburgh, studying chemistry at the University, and, if he did not actually play with his fellow students, must have been aware of their excursions to Musselburgh and North Berwick. There is certainly no doubt that he had an interest in the game early in life, for in 1863, after his marriage to Princess Alexandra of Denmark, he acknowledged a loyal address from the Royal and Ancient Golf Club by consenting to be the club's Patron and announcing his intention of becoming captain.

A club minute for 30 September 1863 stated:

H.R.H. the Prince of Wales, having this day gained the Silver Club (being represented by John Whyte-Melville, Esq., of Strathkinness), Mr. Whyte-Melville, in the name and at the special request of H.R.H., took the Chair as Captain of the Club.

So the future Edward VII did not 'drive himself into office' in the accustomed way, this being done by proxy, but his absence from that ceremony and also from the club's business meetings during his term of office can be explained by pressure of affairs rather than any inability to play or understand the game. This is clear from the fact that during his reign he enjoyed playing on a golf course laid out for him in the Home Park at Windsor.

Thirteen years later the last of Victoria's sons, Prince Leopold, Duke of Albany, became R. and A. captain and drove into office, according to custom, as a minute of September 1876, shows: 'H.R.H. Prince Leopold having this day gained the Silver Club, he was duly installed as Captain of the Club and took the chair accordingly.'

Almost at the same time Prince Leopold's older brother Arthur, Duke of Connaught, became Honorary President of the Musselburgh Golf Club, and two months later gave consent for the use of the 'Royal' prefix.

Later in his life Edward, both as Prince and as King, became patron of several other golf clubs, and in that capacity performed the opening ceremony when the Marienbad club in Austria (now in Czechoslovakia) was started in 1905. Two generations later his grandsons took to golf, the most enthusiastic being Edward Prince of Wales, afterwards Edward VIII and Duke of Windsor, who, not content with being an active captain of several clubs, including the R. and A., played golf in many parts of the world during his frequent tours abroad. He was R. and A. captain in 1922 and his brothers the Duke of York (afterwards George VI) and the Duke of Kent followed his example in 1930 and 1937. All three 'drove into office' and played in the subsequent medal competitions.

The public courses in Richmond Park, Prince's and Duke's, were named after the Prince of Wales and the Duke of York, who performed the respective opening ceremonies. Edward was a keen follower of professional golf and often had lessons from Archie Compston at Coombe Hill, Surrey, where he played occasionally in competitions. He was a spectator at Carnoustie in 1931 when Tommy Armour won the Open Championship, and again at Southport for the Ryder Cup match of 1933, when he handed the trophy to the winning captain, J. H. Taylor. In 1930 he had played in a match at Sunningdale in which his brother the Duke of Kent and the famous American amateur, Bobby Jones, took part.

The Duke of York, who was good enough at lawn tennis to play at Wimbledon, had little time for active participation in sport after ascending the throne, but he retained his interest in golf and in 1948, during an official visit to Edinburgh, spent a day at Muirfield to see Henry Cotton win the Open Championship for the third time.

There was no prince in the next generation and golf could not compete with polo, racing and equestrianism, but the Queen is patron of the Professional Golfers' Association and the many 'Royal' clubs in the country pay testimony to past favours. When the Prince of Wales went to Southport in 1933 many of the 15,000 spectators were there only to see him, and he must have made many converts to golf by his presence alone. Today the star players are given princely adulation by knowledgeable crowds, and it is doubtful if the prospect of seeing a royal personage in the gallery would make any significant difference in the takings.

Many of the 'Royal' clubs abroad provide evidence of patronage by British monarchs—Royal Calcutta, Royal Cape, Royal Melbourne, Royal Hong Kong and Royal Montreal are a few examples —but there are also clubs like Royal Copenhagen, Royal Madrid (or Real Club de la Puerta de Hierro) and several 'Royals' in Belgium to show that foreign kings have favoured the game. In that aspect Belgium is far in advance of any other Continental country. The enthusiasm of King Albert led to the founding of the Royal Golf Club de Belgique in 1906, and no doubt infected his successor, for Leopold III played occasionally in the Belgian Amateur Championship while on the throne. Later, after retiring in favour of his son Baudouin, Leopold reached the quarter-finals of the French Amateur Championship and played in numerous open competitions. King Baudouin himself represented Belgium in an international contest with France and Holland, and also competed with Dai Rees, the Ryder Cup star, in the Gleneagles Hotel amateur-professional foursomes tournament in Perthshire. It is therefore not surprising that eight of Belgium's thirteen golf clubs are 'Royal'. That title is more sparingly used in Britain, where no more than forty clubs out of about 1,500 are authorized. There are obvious difficulties of protocol and security about kings and princes competing in open events. But there has been enough regal interest in golf for many centuries and in many parts of the world to justify the proud title of Royal and Ancient.

CHAPTER 24

The new artisan golfer

Golf was no more immune than any other activity from the changes in human relationships and social conditions caused by the Great War, and the artisan clubs of England were particularly susceptible to the impact of new and democratic ideas. The older ones had started in rural areas in the days when there was almost a feudal relationship between master and man. Most of the artisans worked near the courses where they played, many being employed by members of the parent club, and some by the club itself. In such circumstances they had a general sense of dependence, and not only accepted but welcomed the arrangement by which they worked on the course in return for playing privileges. Artisans in country areas were low-paid and the work-and-play arrangement provided opportunities they would not have had otherwise. They were also hard pressed to afford equipment, and gratefully accepted gifts of used balls and old clubs from the parent members—gifts given and received with no embarrassment on either side.

That state of affairs persisted for a long time in country places, but by the 1920s artisan golf had spread to suburban districts where feudalism had never existed. Wages were higher, working conditions better, and democratic attitudes more pronounced in the towns. The new artisan was able to pay his way at a reasonable level, had no desire to work on the course, and was not disposed to regard as charity the playing privileges offered by the parent club. As the movement spread in the towns, it obtained more recruits from those earning good money in various occupations, and whereas the older country-based clubs tended to continue the work-and-play system, the newer ones sought more equable arrangements. The artisans' main problem was to get playing facilities, and they were able and willing to pay for them. Most artisan clubs now pay annual fees to the parent clubs based on their restricted playing hours. In general they are allowed to start before 9 a.m. and to play at certain times in the evenings, and the annual fees, which vary considerably, are in addition to the individual subscriptions paid by the artisans to their own clubs to cover running costs. This arrangement is mutually satisfactory. The artisans enjoy facilities without feeling dependent, and the parent clubs derive extra revenue for the use of their courses at times when their own members are inactive.

These changes paved the way for a national organization, and the Artisan Golfers' Association was formed in 1921, with Lord Riddell, so long a benefactor to golf, as the first President. The principal object was 'to extend the game, particularly among the working men of England and Wales'. Shortly afterwards a northern section was formed and there is now an Irish AGA with nineteen affiliated clubs. The interest of patrons like Lord Riddell and the Earl of Derby, who became President of the northern section, helped to raise the status of the AGA, and the late Secretary, W. J. Gardner, worked hard for many years to that end. In 1938 the English Golf Union allotted a place on its council for an AGA representative, and after the War, with the help of a Vice-President, Lord Teviot, a past captain of the R. and A., an annual match was promoted between the Artisans and the premier club. Then a similar series was started with the Oxford and Cambridge Golfing Society, and the social barriers of Victorian times had been well and truly breached. Another milestone in the AGA history was reached in 1950 when eight artisans competed in trial matches at Deal so that the Walker Cup selectors could assess their abilities. None was chosen for that match against the United States, but the breakthrough encouraged many good artisans to venture into open competitions and championships. The most successful was Douglas Sewell, then a member of Hook Heath Artisans at Woking, who worked on the Southern Railway. He won the English Amateur Championship in 1958 and 1960, and in each of those years played in the Walker Cup matches. Sewell, who later had a successful career as a professional, was the first member of an AGA club to gain international honours, but not the first artisan to do so. Abe Mitchell, the gardener from Forest Row, Sussex, and a member of the Cantelupe Artisans, played three times for England against Scotland in 1910–11–12 before turning professional.

But when the Walker Cup matches began in 1922, it would have been unprecedented for an artisan to be chosen to play against the United States, the places going to Oxford and Cambridge blues and golfers of a similar social standard. It was not so much a matter of class distinctions as of economics. In those days it was almost impossible for an artisan golfer to play in enough important events to give the selectors a proper idea of his value, and since most of his golf was played in his club circle he had very limited scope for developing his game to international standards. During the last forty years the spread of county golf leading to national golf, the growing independence of artisans and their improved financial circumstances, have combined to bring about great changes and create many more opportunities for artisans to reach international rank. These factors also created subtle changes in the relations between artisans and parent clubs. A typical case concerned Swinley Forest, a very exclusive club with a course on Crown land near Ascot. The members complained that, on arriving for their Sunday morning rounds, they found much of the parking space occupied by the cars of artisans already on the course. They naturally wondered why men who could afford cars should be subsidised by getting virtually free golf. An analysis of the artisan membership showed that while some of them were manual workers the others were members because that was the only way they could play on the private courses in their district. The matter was thrashed out in a friendly atmosphere and the Swinley Forest artisans now willingly pay realistic fees for the privileges received.

Half a century earlier the Royal Ascot club, playing over Ascot Heath, had an arrangement of this kind with local tradesmen and artisans. The attached club was called Ascot St George's and the membership was limited to twenty-five, all carrying on business or working at a trade within three miles of the Grand Stand. In Edwardian days the St George's members paid one guinea a year against the subscription of three guineas paid by members of the parent club.

Most clubs now affiliated to the AGA have similar relations with their parents. The artisans' annual subscriptions average between £15 and £20 a head, and in general it can be assumed that the artisan pays about 25–30 per cent of the parent club subscription. If the latter is about £50 the artisan would be expected to pay about £15. His opportunities for golf are restricted to certain times, but this disadvantage is more than balanced by the benefits. He can play on a first-class course in a club atmosphere and enjoy the society of his fellow-members afterwards, at a cost far below what he would pay on a public course, where he would have to queue for starting times and share the facilities with hundreds of strange players of varying ability and experience. Public course fees in London are approximately 50p per round. For not much more than half that sum weekly the average artisan can get at least two rounds in the winter and much more in the light summer evenings, while enjoying his own type of exclusive club life.

That is one reason why, despite all the changes in social attitudes and the continuous erosion of class distinctions, members of artisan clubs and those of private clubs go on living in different worlds—by choice. The private club golfer is usually one who has never known the artisan world and has no wish to enter it. Not from any snobbish feeling of superiority but because he is geared to the private world and accustomed to finding his fun and his friends there. The artisan is content with his world for similar reasons. Not inverted snobbery but a desire to play golf and enjoy social relaxations with friends in familiar and unrestrained surroundings. I could give many instances of this difference in outlook and inclination, but it will suffice to quote that of the Walton Heath artisans, because they share the pleasures of golf on two of our finest inland courses with members of an exclusive and expensive club, and do so in an atmosphere of mutual trust, independence and amity. The artisans of Walton Heath developed under the kindly interest of Lord Riddell, first President of their Association and for many years the ruling power at the parent club. In his day Walton Heath was the golfing resort of politicians and diplomats, and during and after the Great War many questions of national importance were discussed after a round of golf had produced the correct relaxed conditions. Lloyd George and other Cabinet ministers often played there, and it was the virtual home of the Parliamentary Handicap tournament. But it was also frequently the venue for the PGA match-play Championship, started in 1903 by Sir Emsley Carr and Lord Riddell, then joint owners of the *News of the World*. That sponsorship lasted until 1969, and the end was also the beginning of a crisis situation for Walton Heath members. They saved their club but the cost of survival was high, and membership became more expensive and therefore more restricted.

Through all the years of change Walton Heath artisans pursued their own way, acknowledging the great help received from the parent club but enjoying their own kind of independence. They had their own clubhouse, and in 1973 built a new one on an adjacent site made available by the parent club. This building was erected almost entirely by the spare-time work of the members, who included operatives in most of the trades involved. In this new home, as in the old, they have their own bar, and on any Sunday from eleven a.m. onwards one can see them coming in from the course, having started their rounds when parent club members were sitting down to breakfast or still between the sheets. Soon their clubhouse would be lively with chatter and badinage over pint tankards dispensed by a member taking his turn behind the bar. If a competition had been played, the cards would be handed in and checked and the result announced with the usual rude remarks about the winner's handicap. In one corner the committee members might be discussing business, and at other tables the playing-cards would be out for a few hands of solo whist or rummy before it was time to go home to Sunday dinner.

In its essentials this scene, which can be seen any Sunday morning in nearly two hundred artisan clubs up and down the country, is no different from what goes on in the bars and lounges of the parent club a few yards away. The time of day is different, and the circumstances, but both worlds have their place in the universe of golf. The all-important point is that the artisans are enjoying a particular kind of golf and communal life and have no wish to change anything. This view was made clear in 1973 by Mr William Farley, honorary secretary of the Artisan Golfers' Association, in commenting on complaints by Labour members of Watford Council that the West Herts Golf Club had barred working-class golfers from entering the clubhouse. The complainants, mainly for political reasons, took up the cudgels on behalf of West Herts Artisans, and created a class distinction where none existed by talking of a 'snob barrier'. The reply of the artisans exploded such theories, because they were quite content to pursue their own activities independently of the parent club, although using the same course. 'It is merely a question of natural selection,' Mr Farley was quoted as saying. 'The artisan members at Watford and at more than 180 other clubs are happier with things as they are.'

From time to time artisans are invited to end their separate status and become full members of the parent club. Their frequent refusals are due more to the reasons already given than to financial inability to make the change. Nevertheless, in parts of the country where conditions are favourable there have been mergers. In recent years nearly 50 artisan clubs out of about 250 have ceased affiliation with the AGA for that reason. Most of the mergers have been made possible by a comparatively small difference between the relative subscriptions, so that the artisans were tempted to pay the higher figure in order to get full facilities. But whether a merger has taken place or the artisans have preserved their separate existence on payment of realistic fees, the modern relationship between the two parties has undergone a profound change to the benefit of both. The parent clubs get more revenue, the artisans have more independence, and their movement itself, so far from suffering, has gained in importance and prestige.

CHAPTER 25

The professional emancipated

Soon after Edward Ray, the professional at Oxhey, Hertfordshire, won the US Open Championship in 1920, he was elected an honorary member of his club—an unprecedented event in British golf which caused raised eyebrows in many quarters. Nowadays the majority of club professionals are either honorary members or have the freedom of the clubhouse; and it is not unusual for the membership to be conferred with the appointment. But when the distinction fell on bluff, hearty, pipe-smoking Ted Ray it caused almost a sensation. Although he had been Open Champion in 1912 before winning the American title and was considered the best of fellows by his professional friends, his forthright manner and blunt conversation scarcely fitted into the atmosphere of the average clubhouse lounge. But he was popular with everyone, and the Oxhey members elected him because they liked him and were proud of his achievements.

This break with tradition opened the gates. Members of other clubs realized that they, too, could show appreciation of long service. Taylor, Vardon and Braid, the three most prominent professionals of the pre-war era, were made honorary members of their respective clubs, and very soon the practice had become commonplace. The War had something to do with it, but there had also been a big change in the status of the professional since the days when he was not allowed in any part of the clubhouse save the staff quarters. Even after playing with a member he would return to his shop to eat a sandwich lunch and brew tea on the gas-ring usually used for the gluepot. It was not unknown for eminent players engaged in exhibition matches to be obliged to eat sandwiches and drink beer in the open air between rounds while the members and visitors who had admired their play lunched in the clubhouse.

Situations of this kind survived from the times when professionals were almost entirely recruited from the ranks of caddies and hangers-on, always found on or near the links and prepared to take any job from club-carrying to coaching. They included many rough-and-ready characters with little education, unpolished manners and a tendency to shabbiness in dress. There were exceptions, but the majority were unacceptable in club circles, and many years were to pass before there was any significant change in the attitude of the amateur towards the professional. Even such men as Robertson, Tom Morris and the elder Park were the servants of the amateurs and conducted themselves accordingly. The twenty years' reign of Vardon, Braid and Taylor was a period of change, and when Abe Mitchell turned professional in 1912 after reaching the Amateur Championship final, he unconsciously set a trend which, many years later, became a regular pattern. Mitchell was twenty-five when he became a professional, and was the first golfer to do so after attaining international rank as an amateur. James Braid remained one till he was twenty-six, but his amateur successes were only in minor events, for those were the days before international matches.

Despite the growing tendency to regard professional golf as a respectable occupation, the idea that a professional's place was outside the clubhouse persisted for a long time in many quarters. Nowadays, when professionals play in the Open Championship at Troon, Muirfield and Hoylake, to name three of the erstwhile ultra-exclusive clubs, they share equally with amateur competitors in the use of the clubhouse; but seniors among them can remember days when they were barred from all clubs on the championship list. When Walter Hagen, the great American golfer who won the Open four times, made his first appearance in Britain in 1920 at Deal, he changed into his golf clothes in a hired car, parked near the clubhouse from which he was excluded, rather than use the overcrowded professional's shop which was the only dressing-room for non-amateurs. The gesture had no visible effect and five years later, during preparations for the Open at Prestwick, a suggestion that part of the clubhouse be set aside for professionals, who had previously had to use a marquee outside, was not well received by the older members of the club. But times were changing, and the sub-committee in charge of the arrangements persuaded the club to provide dressing-room accommodation in the building. Despite this relaxation the professionals were critical of the general arrangements, and their Association made representations to the R. and A. Championship Committee demanding better conditions at future championships. Today no clubhouse is barred to professional competitors on such occasions, and no one could quibble at the reasonable wish of the local members to reserve part of the building for their exclusive use.

Golf, indeed, was passing through a transition period which was affecting other sports. While professional golfers were becoming restive about restrictions based on class distinctions, the cricketing public were growing critical of such snobbish customs as giving professionals' surnames only in the printed score-sheets, and using separate gates at Lord's for the respective teams in the Gentlemen *v.* Players match. The eventual disappearance of these and other sporting demarcations reflected not only changing social attitudes but also a rise in the status of professionals, and this was particularly the case with golf. At one time almost the only way into the professional's shop led from the caddie's shed, but between the wars a new generation arrived bred on different ideas. Henry Cotton, three times Open Champion, son of a successful business man, was a member of a private club while at Alleyn's School, Dulwich. He played only once, and without distinction, in the Boys' Amateur Championship at the age of fourteen, and left school at seventeen to be an assistant professional. Two years later he secured his first appointment as full professional, and developed into the most successful British golfer of his generation. Since then his example has been followed by many young golfers, expensively educated, who might have chosen careers in commerce or the professions instead of deciding to earn a living on the links; and the successful young amateur of the 1970s is almost expected to turn professional, instead of being criticized for so doing.

These developments have been due partly to the big increase in the number of prize-money tournaments and the value of the rewards. For the first thirty years of its existence the Professional Golfers' Association was conducted almost like a trade union, dedicated to the welfare of the club professional. Tournaments were few in number, with small prizes, and the PGA administration played a comparatively passive part in promoting them. In 1933 a retired Royal Navy officer, Commander R. C. T. Roe, became PGA Secretary and, appreciating the potentialities of tournaments and international contests, set out to make the Association a vital force in world golf. During the twenty-five years of his reign the tournament programme developed extensively, and the Association now has a high-powered organization controlling events worth well over half a million pounds. Inevitably the character of the professional player has changed. At one time he played in the rare competitions almost as a relief from the daily round of tasks at his home club. Now the big prizes are contested by men whose activities are directed solely at winning tournaments, and have neither the ability nor the desire to be club professionals involved in teaching and shopkeeping.

The club professional is still very important, and at his best can flourish to an extent which makes his career much more lucrative than that of many tournament players who fail to reach the top grade. Despite the increase in the value of tournaments the really big prizes are shared by only a few professionals. For example, the world-wide earnings of two hundred players of all nationalities in the whole of 1972 totalled approximately £3,600,000 and £1,400,000 of that was pocketed by the first twenty-four in the list. Only the first hundred exceeded £10,000 in winnings and the two hundredth made no more than £4,000. An even bleaker picture is produced by recent statistics of prize money in Britain; and the great majority of those who play in tournaments are in constant danger of failing to get an income big enough to offset the considerable expenses involved and provide a good living. The successful club professional, on the other hand, can look forward to a lifetime of service to appreciative club members.

Many tournament players do hold genuine club appointments and employ assistants to run their shops during absences. But the extent and richness of the modern tournament schedule, at home and abroad, has made it almost mandatory for the professional to choose between a club job and a freelance playing existence. The two do not mix easily.

CHAPTER 26

Jews in golf clubs

Golf clubs, no matter how, why or where they were formed, all possess the right to decide who should be admitted to membership. This power of acceptance or rejection is not confined to golf; it still has its place in the customs, if not in the rules, of practically all private organizations. In Victorian and Edwardian times, when social standing was all-important and upper-class snobbery at its height, the black ball reigned supreme. In many cases one black ball in the ballot box was sufficient to exclude. Other clubs were more indulgent. But in most instances the candidate who had had the misfortune to incur the enmity or antipathy of one or more members could not gain admission, even if sponsored by existing members of acceptable character. Sometimes neither enmity nor dislike was involved. An aversion born of instinct, a touchy liver or the ghost of a rumour might be equally damaging to the applicant's chances. The great injustice of the black ball system is that the ballot is secret and enables an anonymous minority to defeat the wishes of the majority. There are other methods of ensuring control over membership intake which may not be much more democratic but do give candidates a sporting chance. One system adopted by several leading clubs requires a minimum number of signatures in support of a nomination, and if that number has not been reached within a set period after a candidate's name has been posted, his application fails out of hand. If the support is adequate it goes before the committee. This method, diametrically opposed to the black ball procedure, puts the emphasis on acceptance, not rejection. If the candidate is known to and respected by enough members he becomes eligible, no matter what may be in the minds of a few disgruntled, apathetic or liverish members who would otherwise shelter in the secrecy of the ballot box.

The general procedure in most golf clubs does not require supporting signatures. It is usual for the candidate's name and those of proposer and seconder to be placed on the notice-board, and he is invited to make use of course and clubhouse until the next committee meeting. In the interval he plays with his sponsors, is introduced to and plays with other members and, if he is wise, makes himself agreeable and discreetly hospitable in the clubhouse. In theory this ensures that no one is elected who is wanting in desirable attributes; in practice it works erratically. But whatever the method, the object is always the same—to keep out undesirables. Naturally there are varying standards of acceptability. Some clubs with membership lists reading like pages from Debrett strive to maintain an exalted tone. Others close their doors to applicants engaged in trade or commerce. Sometimes the popularity of the course dictates an ultra-selective policy; equally there are many clubs so short of members that they will accept almost anyone. But all have the power of rejection and use it in various ways. It is rare nowadays to find a club in a populous district which does not have a waiting list. Sometimes it actually exists on paper—names of applicants waiting for vacancies; more often it is an abstract device for avoiding direct rejection. To be refused membership out of hand is a blow to one's self-esteem; to be put 'on the waiting list' lacks the cruel touch of finality. The result in both cases is often the same but the stratagem is kinder to the feelings and, more importantly, cannot be challenged.

Although a snobbish exclusiveness can still be observed in a few clubs of real or fancied importance, the great majority have more tolerant attitudes and a genuine waiting list is demanded by extremely practical considerations. Nearly all clubs in and around towns and cities fix maximum figures for full members, depending on the number who can be accommodated comfortably at peak periods during week-ends. Clubs with more than one course, or single-course clubs able to use a number of alternative starting-points, are able to extend their lists, but clubs with none of those advantages would be hard pressed to exceed three hundred full members. They can elect a limited number of five-day members who cannot play at week-ends except on payment of a green fee; and lady members bring the total average membership to five hundred. This gives a total of about 750,000 golfers belonging to clubs, and as it is estimated that British golfers now total well in excess of a million, it cannot be denied that existing playing facilities are grossly inadequate. Inevitably the commitee of a club will fill vacancies in a selective way, having regard not to the applicant's position on the waiting list but to other factors, including pressure from existing members to influence choice in favour of their friends or relatives. Preference is often given to family connections, to candidates already friendly with a number of members, and to those with short handicaps or sufficiently experienced to be well past the beginner stage.

The growing popularity of golf which outstripped the capacity of existing clubs was one cause of the discrimination against Jews which was rife between the wars and led to the establishment of many 'Jewish clubs' now scattered around the country. Jews are now among the keenest golfers, but their interest is of fairly recent growth, and due probably to the development of suburban golf in the 1890s and the fact that Jews are mainly town-dwellers.

When golf became popular enough to attract business men, traders and industrialists who built courses in their neighbourhoods, it also attracted Jews living in the same communities. But for various reasons many of these new golf clubs either shut the doors completely to Jews or admitted them cautiously. Time has softened attitudes and there is more tolerance today, but between the World Wars Jewish golfers in certain localities with large Jewish communities found it often impossible, and at the best rather difficult, to gain admission to a club. The argument in many committee rooms seems to have run on these lines: 'We think he's a nice chap and a sportsman. He's played with several members and no one has a bad word to say against him. But if we let him in he'll bring in his pals who might not be so agreeable, and before long they'll be running the club and entering into expensive innovations. Up will go the subscriptions and it won't be the same old club.'

These observations were confirmed to a great extent by an exhaustive investigation carried out in 1960 by the *Jewish Chronicle*. One of the conclusions arrived at was that, although many clubs practised overt or hidden discrimination, there was a far greater number who admitted members without regard to race or religion. Significantly, the clubs unwilling to accept Jews, or adopting a quota system, were mainly in the areas of considerable Jewish population, notably in North London and big provincial cities like Leeds, Manchester, Birmingham, Glasgow and Liverpool. The journal's investigators made particular reference to the experiences of two ladies living in Hampstead and Golders Green in north London during two years of efforts to join a club. They were turned down, sometimes openly but in other cases subtly by a dozen clubs. The usual excuse was 'no vacancies', the ladies' section of a club often becoming mysteriously filled as soon as the committee members became aware of the applicants' religion. At one club one of the ladies was told by the secretary that if Jews were accepted there would be no room for ordinary people.

Among the reasons given for discrimination by quota was the fear that uncontrolled admission would lead to a predominance of Jewish members. Another reason was that Jewish golfers had a different outlook on life, different ideas on running a club, and modest drinking habits. Since most golf clubs depend heavily on bar profits, there is a practical reason for unwillingness to admit too many Jews. One outcome in the 1920s was the formation of golf clubs either all-Jewish or Jewish-controlled. Most of them have high subscriptions, partly to finance an extravagant and ostentatious environment, but also to compensate for comparatively low bar receipts. Soon after the Second World War, when rationing of spirits was still in force, I visited Potters Bar, where practically all the three hundred members were Jews, and was surprised to have no trouble in buying a tot of whisky. The steward explained that the consumption of spirits was so small that the club's quota of six bottles of whisky a month was more than sufficient! Jews generally do not indulge to any great extent in intoxicating liquor, but they are generous to guests, can be relied upon to finance the needs of their clubs if the subscriptions prove inadequate, and are enthusiastic contributors to charitable enterprises concerning their own race.

One of the difficulties in the past has been the conflict between the flamboyant and luxurious tastes of Jewish golfers and the comparatively conservative attitude of Gentile club members. Having visited many Jewish clubs over a period of many years, I know that generally they are run more efficiently than the majority of other clubs. This is not surprising having regard for the keen business instincts of Jews. Whereas the ordinary golfer is content to enjoy his game and not worry much about how the business of the club is conducted (so long as his subscription remains modest), the Jew is deeply interested in administration and finance. It follows that any Gentile club admitting Jews in large numbers would be likely to find life more difficult and more expensive.

Some of the differences mentioned are beyond elimination, and therefore the creation of all-Jewish clubs, or clubs with a majority of Jewish members, has seemed to be a logical and even desirable solution. This trend began in 1920, when the Moor Allerton club was started on the northern outskirts of Leeds, a city with a large number of Jewish residents, engaged mostly in the clothing trade. The present Moor Allerton clubhouse, opened in 1971, is a show place, but the club started modestly enough with a converted farmhouse as quarters and amenities which compared unfavourably with those of private clubs in the same neighbourhood. In 1921 the Whitefields club was instituted in Manchester, and in 1923 a syndicate of north London Jews began operations at Potters Bar. The trend was continued after the Second World War, beginning in 1946 with the purchase of Coombe Hill course and clubhouse in Surrey by another association of Jewish golfers. There are now twelve clubs affiliated to the National Association of Jewish Golf Clubs and Societies, the other being Hartsbourne (Herts.), Edmondstown (Dublin), Lee Park (Liverpool), Shirley (Birmingham), Bonnyton (Glasgow), Dunham Forest (Manchester), Abridge (Essex) and Dyrham Park (Herts). The last three were created from scratch on virgin soil and on very modern lines, replete with up-to-date amenities; but in those ventures Jewish golfers were merely following the general move towards more sophisticated facilities. Few golfers in these days are averse to enjoying all the available comforts which can be provided inside and outside the clubhouse, and for many years we have seen successive increases in subscriptions and the provision of indoor appointments which in quality and range would have been deemed unnecessary, even unseemly, by players of Victorian times. It has taken three generations for golfers to free themselves from the primitive simplicity of tin huts, wooden pavilions, enamel wash-basins and 'men only' bars, and embrace whole-heartedly and easily the idea of mansion clubhouses, showers, lounges, mixed bars and ladies' powder-rooms. Jewish clubs which started half a century ago did so on simple lines consistent with the times. Those that are now regarded in some quarters as opulent and ostentatious have merely kept up with the times and, for every one of those, there are a score or more of non-Jewish clubs operated on equally high standards. Another point which must be made is that most Jewish clubs welcome visitors without introduction, and only one has a definite rule requiring introduction by a member at all times. There are also several cases of Gentiles serving on the committees of these clubs and even of non-Jewish captains.

The problem has always been most difficult in areas of large Jewish population, and has been solved to a great extent by the establishment of Jewish clubs. Elsewhere, which means in the great majority of clubs, there is no evidence of intolerance, and in higher social circles admission has never been based on race or religion, but on suitability in other respects. The Royal and Ancient Golf Club of St Andrews has several Jewish members; so have the Oxford and Cambridge Golfing Society and various other associations of golfers having common interests.

The Association of Jewish Golf Clubs and Societies, formed in 1949, has objects quite unconnected with combating discrimination, and takes no part in controversy on that subject. It exists to assist in the formation of Jewish clubs, to arrange matches between them, run competitions, and organize charitable efforts. Most individual Jews, when questioned by the *Jewish Chronicle* investigators, deplored any attempt to publicize charges of discrimination, and took the view that all clubs are entitled to do as they please. Captain W. G. L. Folkard, at that time Secretary of the English Golf Union, was quoted as saying, 'A golf club is the extension of one's home; the election of new members is a purely domestic matter.'

CHAPTER 27

Golf for all ages

Of the many changes in the golf landscape over the last fifty years none has been more remarkable, or more significant for the future, than the advance in the status of the teenager. From being scarcely tolerated by his elders, he has become important in the eyes of many adults now actively and enthusiastically concerned in the training and encouragement of juniors. And the keenness of the organizers has been matched by that of the youngsters. Ever since golf began, young people have played, but only in recent times have they had the benefit of systematic tuition. Our grandfathers and great-grandfathers, when young, learned almost in spite of adult indifference. They acquired skill naturally, largely by imitation, and the best became good players because they had inherent aptitude. But in extreme youth they had to defer to their elders on the links, as elsewhere. At most clubs juniors were not allowed on the main course and were far from welcome on the ladies' course. They had to play in odd corners and odd times and be wary of getting in the way. Yet when they became adult in turn, they tended to forget the trials of their youth and treated the next generation with equal indifference, bordering on intolerance. Another big obstacle was the rigid opposition by most headmasters. Boys and girls from golfing families found that golf was frowned on in term-time because, in the view of opponents, it was a selfish game, whereas football and cricket were character-building games which cultivated the team spirit. That was the general attitude of schoolmasters outside Scotland, where the game was too firmly entrenched in tradition to be shunned by anyone.

Golf was not entirely discouraged at English schools. Eton College had a team in the 1920s, and when Stowe School was founded in Buckinghamshire in 1926, golf was an important part of the sports curriculum. Stowe had its own course, laid out in the park belonging to the historic mansion, and two boys who profited by the facilities to become Walker Cup internationals were P. B. (Laddie) Lucas and John Langley. Lucas had had a sound grounding in extreme youth, for his father helped to lay out the Prince's links at Sandwich and was first secretary of the club. Lucas played there from childhood and achieved a hole in one at the age of ten. Although he was not a product of Stowe School golf, he influenced the growth of the game there, as did A. Stanley Anderson, a Stowe master and a leading amateur player. Langley was a true product of Stowe and proved the value of that early experience when, in 1936, aged only eighteen and holder of the Boys' Amateur Championship title, he reached the final of the English Amateur Championship at Deal.

By that time many people in authority were tackling the problem of providing proper tuition for the young. For many years there had been annual competitions and championships which provided opportunities for the best teenagers to gain experience, but these, like so many other innovations in golf, sprang from unofficial sources and were much later taken up by the ruling bodies. The Boys' Championship was founded in 1921 by a private individual, Lt.-Col. T. H. South, and organized by the Royal Ascot Club. Two years afterwards, Mr D. M. Mathieson, father of the first Boy Champion, became chairman of an organizing committee, and the event rapidly increased in importance and appeal as it was taken to various fine courses in England and Scotland. After twenty-five years of progress interrupted by the Second World War, the Championship passed under the control of the Royal and Ancient Golf Club and now forms part of the official programme.

The Girls' Championship had a similar history. It was planned for 1914, and among those who entered was Joyce Wethered, then fourteen and destined to be the greatest woman golfer of her generation. The Great War intervened, and when the Girls' Championship was decided for the first time in 1919, for a trophy given by a magazine, the *Gentlewoman*, Miss Wethered was too old to compete. Instead she won nine senior national championships in ten years. The Girls' Championship was taken over by another magazine, the *Bystander*, in 1925, but after the Second World War the proprietors gave their trophy to the Ladies' Golf Union and the championship was revived in 1949 as an official LGU event. The original *Gentlewoman* trophy had been given to the Lady Golfers' Club many years before, but was stolen from the Golfers' Club premises in St James's in 1972.

Everyone having the interests of golf at heart was now well aware of the importance of encouraging youth, and the climate was favourable for a positive move—the formation in 1952 of Golf Foundation Ltd, a non-profit-making body devoted to the teaching of schoolboys and schoolgirls. Progress was slow at first, due partly to lack of funds and partly to indifference and even hostility in some quarters, notably among schoolmasters. But the enthusiasm of the pioneers overcame prejudice, and very quickly the great enterprise got into top gear to develop at ever-increasing momentum. In 1973, when it came of age, Golf Foundation could report on magnificent progress from very modest beginnings. In its first year sixty boys attended classes, and they represented only six schools. Now there are 1,600 schools involved, and each year about 30,000 more boys and girls are introduced to golf through the Foundation classes.

The professionals conducting Golf Foundation classes also encourage support from their members by arranging special competitions in Golf Foundation Week, an annual enterprise which, together with the annual Golf Ball, produces much-needed revenue. The finances also receive great support from firms in the golf trade, and while this is of course due principally to the vested interests involved, the executives of such firms who have seats on the Golf Foundation council give a lot of their spare time to achieving the best results. The professionals who came into the scheme originally in an experimental mood were soon imbued with enthusiasm. They receive only modest fees for the mass tuition they provide, but have the satisfaction of knowing they are providing a steady increase in the number of well-taught recruits to a game on which their livelihood depends. It must be added, however, that Golf Foundation Week is supported by only about 300 clubs out of 1,800 in Britain. In this, as in so many ventures, a few dedicated and interested people are doing good work in an otherwise largely indifferent world.

In recent years several significant developments have widened the scope for junior training. They include county schools' associations with programmes of inter-county matches; a British and Irish team championship for boys, contested in 1974 by 420 schools; and the institution of open coaching centres during school holidays. There is also a scheme for giving special tuition to youngsters who show great promise. All this has had an immense effect on the quality of entrants to professional golf. Formerly the professional either graduated from the ranks of caddies, having taught himself by imitation, or became an assistant on leaving school without having had the benefit of organized coaching. But the boy trained under the Golf Foundation scheme, and being able to compete in many junior competitions and inter-county matches, or, if he is good enough, achieving junior international rank, has two alternatives. He can still become an assistant while in his teens, with the opportunity of taking part in the PGA training scheme. Or he can continue playing as an amateur until he gains some distinction, and then turn professional.

Of course a boy with great potential can break through in any circumstances, as can be seen by comparing the careers of Britain's two best players of the seventies. Tony Jacklin, Open Champion in 1969 and winner of the United States Open Championship in 1970 (he held both titles at the same time) was not a product of Golf Foundation. He went straight from school to be an assistant at a London club, Potters Bar, and worked his way to the front as many famous players had done before him. Peter Oosterhuis, who achieved a British record by finishing third in the US Masters' tournament and ended that season by topping the British averages for the third successive year, was trained under Golf Foundation, played in the Walker Cup match while still a public school pupil, and so was rich in quality and experience before he turned professional.

Oosterhuis's case provides an interesting sidelight on the changes in social attitudes during the past twenty-five years. In the old days a golfer who built up a reputation as a first-class amateur usually remained an amateur, for two reasons. He almost always belonged to an upper-class or middle-class community and having been educated for a career in business or one of the professions, had neither the need nor the inclination to play golf for a living, since to become a professional was to subside into a subservient position in relation to club members. The other reason was that the Professional Golfers' Association had a rule compelling any adult who turned professional to wait five years before being able to play in PGA tournaments. Jack McLean, who played many times for Scotland and twice for Britain against the United States before turning professional in 1936; and Eric Brown, who did so at the age of twenty-one after winning the Scottish amateur title, were among those affected. Brown, once the period of restriction was over, began a tournament career of marked success and played in four Ryder Cup matches. But McLean, who was older than Brown when he made the break, never achieved prominence as a tournament player, although very successful as a club professional.

The five-year rule, imposed by professionals fearing damage to their calling through an influx of accomplished amateurs who had not been trained in the professional's shop, could not survive the changing circumstances of the 1950s. It gave way to one which allowed any amateur to turn professional before the age of twenty-five, with a proviso that he would have to wait six months before being eligible for money prizes in PGA tournaments. The way was then open for any ambitious youngster to establish himself by playing for his country or winning a national title, and then embracing professional golf with all the opportunities offered. The six months' wait was scarcely a hindrance, for the amateur could announce his change of status in October or November and be eligible for prize money at the start of the next British season.

It is now almost commonplace for an amateur of international rank to become a professional. No eyebrows are raised, as they would have been half a century ago. The case of Abe Mitchell, who took the step immediately after playing in the Amateur Championship final in 1912, concerned an artisan golfer who appreciated the possibilities of getting a better living from golf. During the next forty years, only two amateurs who had played in British Walker Cup teams turned professional—Jack McLean in 1936 and another Scot, Hector Thomson, in 1940. But during the twelve years from 1960 to 1971 there were twelve cases. A very similar pattern was followed in the United States where, in the same 1960–71 period more than twenty golfers became professionals after achieving international rank as amateurs. The most celebrated of these were Arnold Palmer, the US Amateur Champion in 1954, and Jack Nicklaus, who won that title in 1959 and 1961. Opportunities for young golfers have always been more plentiful in the United States than in Britain, for many American high schools have their golf squads, there is a proliferation of inter-collegiate events, and the Public Links Championship, which annually attracts an entry of about 3,000, has a team section which gives many promising teen-agers their chance to prove themselves.

Nevertheless, Britain is rapidly approaching a situation in which she can bear comparison with the United States. Seventy years ago, few boys from working-class families had any prospect of entering golf save as caddies first and—sometimes—professionals later. Nowadays any keen boy can learn golf in an organized way, can receive help in equipping himself, and be encouraged by school authorities and county unions. There are many adult golfers in positions of influence and authority who devote much time at their own expense to ensure that talent is found and developed on the right lines. Their attitude is far different from that of their grand-fathers. By their efforts, helped by the publicity now lavished on golf and by the performances of the great ones, the modern junior is made ambitious, and ambition is the driving force behind the success of the stars. The path to efficiency and affluence has been made easier and the game assured of a constant flow of new, healthy blood.

While so much is being done for the young, the needs of adult beginners are not being neglected. At one time the mature business man who had had no time for golf while making his way in the world took up the game in later life by joining a club and having lessons from the professional. The sporting man who played foot-ball and cricket in his prime turned to golf in his forties and usually did well because of his good ball sense. But in both cases the interest was awakened by golfing friends and relations, and the initiation made easy. Nowadays there is a constant and increasing influx of adult beginners who have no golfing background, no friends or relations to smooth the path to club membership. They are from all classes and occupations and have become interested by watching big golf on television or by playing on seaside pitch-and-putt courses during holidays. Having a desire to get practical experi-ence, they face the problem of starting. Membership of a private club is next to impossible and a public course far too public for taking first steps. The need produced solutions. On the one side various commercial concerns developed driving ranges which could be used in all weathers and by night as well as in daylight, the larger golf centres including par-three courses and other attrac-tions. On the other side, mass tuition classes were run by many municipal authorities as well as by the Central Council for Physical Recreation and its Scottish counterpart.

For small fees, often only a few shillings per session, adults could go to classes attended by other pupils in the same stage of experi-ence, and learn without embarrassment, or, by attending a driving range and hiring golf balls by the bucket, they could receive tuition from resident professionals. Most golf centres now have licensed restaurants and lounges, and regular customers tend to gather at regular times, so developing a pleasant and familiar social atmosphere. The golf beginner who has to work all day can use the facilities in the evening under cover, and most of the municipal and CCPR classes are also held indoors and in the evenings. By these means thousands of men and women are being introduced to golf every year who otherwise would have found it impossible to get practical experience under the right conditions.

The problem of teaching beginners of all ages has been solved. But the problem of providing them with playing room remains. It cannot be solved entirely by the golf centres and mass classes, valuable though they are. Golf can reach fruition only on full-length courses, and the supply is still lagging well behind demand.

CHAPTER 28

Professional power

As the world in general embraced twen-
tieth-century ideas of democratic equality and interdependence, so
the world of golf broke away from the class-conscious straitjacket of
Victorian and Edwardian times. Any of the several bodies representing different sections of the golf community—secretaries,
stewards, green-keepers, professionals, artisans and journalists—
can make approaches to higher authority or be called into consul-
tation on important issues; but any such situation, even if organization on that scale had existed before the Great War, could not have
been imagined then. The early history of the Professional Golfers'
Association, born in the first year of Edward VII's reign, shows
clearly the difference between the pre-war and post-war attitudes
of the ruling class. The PGA is now a powerful and influential body
with more than 1,500 members and a tournament programme
worth more than half a million pounds. But it started as a trade
union with the prime aim of protecting the interests of members
and ensuring their welfare. One of the objects, it is true, was to hold
competitions, but that took second place for many years to the
preservation of communal well-being. The members had no say in
the government of golf, which was entirely in the hands of amateurs
not disposed to brook interference from outside bodies, least of all
professionals. Most of the competitors in the Open Championship
were professionals, but for sixty years they were given no chance of
sharing in the arrangements for an event which depended so much
on their efforts and performances.

The first attempt by professionals to assert themselves ante-dated
the PGA by two years. On the eve of the 1899 Championship at
Sandwich, many players threatened to withdraw unless the prize
money was increased. The attempt failed mainly because none of

the leading professionals, including Vardon, Braid and Taylor, would have anything to do with it, but the threat had some effect for the first prize was increased from £40 to £50 and the second from £20 to £25.

In 1907 the PGA, concerned about the increasing difficulty of completing the Open in two days with all the competitors playing in every round, proposed to the six clubs concerned in the organization that there should be a two-day qualifying test with only sixty players going forward to the championship itself. These representations fell on deaf ears, but three years later the Open was extended to three days, with a reduced field for the last 36 holes on the final day, and in 1912 the championship clubs introduced pre-qualifying rounds. This belated agreement with the PGA suggestions did not indicate any intention to consider either the wishes of the professionals or their welfare. It was dictated by a big increase in the number of entries. The arrangements for each championship remained in the hands of the host club and, although circumstances varied, the effect for the professionals was the same—they had to fend for themselves.

This neglect was tolerable at St Andrews where hotels and boarding-houses abounded within a few yards of the course, but at some other courses professionals denied access to the clubhouses often had uncomfortable changing-quarters and feeding facilities which depended on the capacity of a local caterer setting up shop in a tent.

From the time that the R. and A. took over control of the Open Championship in 1920, circumstances gradually improved. In June of the previous year a conference of delegates representing the championship clubs and the PGA met to discuss resumption of the Open, and henceforth the R. and A. always welcomed suggestions by the professionals, while refusing all attempts by the PGA to have a seat on the Championship Committee. This was a reasonable refusal, because the Committee deals also with the Amateur Championship and other events with which the professionals are not concerned.

Prior to the 1925 Open Championship at Prestwick the PGA sent delegates to a meeting of the Championship Committee and evidently strong representations were made about accommodation for the professionals, because the Prestwick Club, for the first time, set aside a locker-room for their use in the clubhouse. On the last occasion, in 1914, they had had to use a marquee pitched outside.

In 1926, when the United States Golf Association legalized the use of steel shafts, the PGA informed the R. and A. that the introduction of these to Britain would be to the detriment of professionals' business. This was so much in line with conservative R. and A. opinion against a big departure from tradition that steel shafts were not legalized. In April 1929, having heard that the R. and A. were considering allowing steel shafts because of the great shortage of hickory, the PGA confirmed their original view that such a move would be against the interests of golf in general and the craft of the club-maker in particular. Nevertheless the R. and A. in the following November legalized steel shafts, and the decision was taken without reference to the PGA. There was a similar lack of liaison in connection with Anglo-American negotiations on a standard golf ball.

This tendency by authority to disregard the opinions of professionals was emphasized a few years later when, in 1937, the USGA and the R. and A. were considering limiting to fourteen the number of clubs which could be used by one player in a competition. A regulation of this kind had become necessary owing to the practice among manufacturers of making clubs in half-sizes, which tended to introduce too much precision into the game and also increased considerably the number of clubs used. For example, in addition to a no. 2 and a no. 3 iron the player could have a no. $2\frac{1}{2}$, the loft of which would be midway between that of the other two clubs. With eight irons at his disposal the golfer would have a difference of about ten yards in the distance obtained by successive clubs. With half-sizes the difference in length of shot from one club to another was reduced to about five yards. In the view of the amateur rule-makers there were three main objections to half-sizes—they made the game easier than it ought to be, created heavy loads for caddies, and tended to involve golfers in more expense.

For obvious reasons professionals took a different view, and the PGA strongly represented to the R. and A. that the proposed legislation was absolutely unnecessary and undesirable. But the R. and A. and the USGA, rightly believing that the interests of the game must be served rather than the interests of professionals, went ahead with the new regulations.

Nevertheless, the climate was changing. The R. and A. Championship Committee, while still not permitting direct PGA representation, was inclined more and more to consult professionals on matters affecting them. For example, when St Andrews wished to change the number of qualifiers for the 1938 Open Championship, the proposals were submitted to the PGA for approval. At about the same time, the R. and A. gave £300 to the PGA funds. These and other signs pointed to the full co-operation which now exists between the two parties. The PGA is in frequent touch with St Andrews over such matters as reinstatement to amateur status, championship conditions and arrangements, and the rules of golf. The Championship Committee and the Rules of Golf Committee remain entirely amateur bodies, mainly because they deal with many matters of purely amateur importance; while the professionals are left to manage their own affairs through the PGA, which has a large secretariat, manages projects involving the expenditure of many thousands of pounds annually, and enjoys a prestige equal to that of any other governing body in the game.

The annual dinner of the PGA is one of the most important events in the world of golf. The Association entertains all the tournament sponsors and many other important guests, including the captain of the Royal and Ancient Golf Club. Individual PGA members make up parties of their club members, and 1200 gleaming shirt fronts under the chandeliers in one of London's biggest hotels emphasize the fact that the PGA of the 1970s is a powerful organization, a long way removed from the days when the professional was more often than not a green-keeper as well, and was not *persona grata* in the clubhouse or the homes of the members he served.

CHAPTER 29

The government of golf

Golf had been played in Britain for five centuries before the spread beyond Scotland to all levels of society produced the need for a central government. The proliferation of clubs in many parts of the British Isles demanded this, for if all the clubs were allowed to pursue their own inclinations in rules and other points of procedure chaos would reign. But the progress towards control by one body was slow and devious. Most golfers who now accept the authority of the Royal and Ancient Golf Club are not aware that this eminence was arrived at very gradually and not fully attained until well into the present century. Of course the influence of St Andrews had been felt for many years before, and it was the tacit acceptance of this fact by otherwise independent clubs and other organizations which led finally to the acknowledgment by all players in Britain, the Commonwealth and many foreign countries of a situation essentially British in its incongruity.

The Americans, whose organization is on an equal footing with that of St Andrews, made a different and characteristic approach to the matter. Only six years after the first American club started, the United States Golf Association was founded in 1894, and quickly gained the allegiance of all players and clubs. Since then the USGA has enjoyed unquestioned authority in that country because it is democratically representative of all ranks.

Need for a central government in Britain was most strongly felt in the matter of rules. The first written regulations were those drawn up for the first competition at Leith in 1744 and adopted almost without alteration by St Andrews ten years later. Before then it had not been necessary, in communities where all players were known to each other and competed only in matches, for everything to be spelt out. The fact that a man was accepted as a member of the

Leith Company or the St Andrews Society was sufficient guarantee that he would adhere to the accepted code of behaviour on the links. The inexorable rule that the ball had to be played as it lay or the hole conceded covered most incidents which could nowadays be the subject of disputes and uncertainties; and, since the matches were between those well acquainted with each other and the links on which they played, there was tacit understanding about procedure and courses of action. Undoubtedly there was a good deal of give-and-take, and some players were sharper than others at gaining the advantage, but while only one match at a time was concerned golfers were quite well able to do without written rules. The start of competitions produced new circumstances. A system adequate for the occasional dispute arising from a match between friends was inadequate for a competition in which the fortunes of everyone, and not of two sides, determined the result. Hence the production of the Leith rules. St Andrews, as we have seen, adopted those rules virtually word-for-word, but as other clubs came into existence each formulated rules controlling the local competitions and necessarily providing for local conditions and possibilities which would not arise in other places. All these early rules therefore varied from each other, and this was not really important while clubs remained few in number and golfers did not often stray from their home courses. But as clubs grew more numerous and transport systems improved, thereby facilitating visits by golfers to neighbouring courses, there was growing dissatisfaction with the existence of many different codes. There were endless disagreements due to the diverse views of golfers in open competitions, coming from different clubs and having to conform to strange rules. The general acceptance by Scottish clubs of the amended and extended St Andrews rules around the middle of the nineteenth century did little to ease matters, because several clubs in England continued to operate under their own rules. Even the Honourable Company had its own code distinct from St Andrews, while most English golfers followed the rules of Wimbledon or Blackheath.

In 1882 St Andrews made still further alterations and additions in the attempt to establish a code acceptable to all, but Blackheath, Wimbledon and the Honourable Company remained uninterested. Six years later St Andrews produced rules which satisfied the dissidents, but neither these nor another set issued in 1892 had any legislative force. In 1896 an effort was made to provide teeth by forming a committee acknowledged by everyone, and unanimity seemed as far off as ever when the English clubs wanted a body composed partly of R. and A. members and partly of representatives of other clubs; whereas the Scottish clubs insisted that it must be wholly R. and A. Eventually the Scottish view was accepted, and in 1897 the first Rules of Golf Committee, consisting of fifteen R. and A. members, was established. It was declared to be the final authority on any question relating to the interpretation of existing rules and customs, but any proposal to amend, repeal or make rules had to be endorsed by a two-thirds majority of R. and A. members at a general meeting.

The effects of this agreement were far-reaching and for the first time golf had a recognized ruling body, since control of the rules meant virtual control of the game. Nevertheless it would have been impossible in the light of later events, particularly relations with the United States, if the Rules of Golf Committee had continued to be composed solely of R. and A. members. Those most concerned saw the wisdom of widening the field as much as possible and eminent golfers outside the R. and A., who possessed considerable influence and experience in the subject, were invited to serve. The committee now consists of twelve members of the R. and A. and eight representatives of other bodies, including the United States Golf Association, the European Golf Association, the British Golf Unions Advisory Council, and ruling bodies of the major Commonwealth countries.

After more than 150 years of rule-making and nearly fifty years of dissension, the R. and A. was confirmed as the supreme authority in that field. But full overlordship was still two decades away, for the Open and Amateur Championships were each controlled by a consortium of clubs until after the Great War. The Open Championship from 1860 to 1870 was handled solely by the Prestwick club, which had provided the Challenge Belt. From 1872 to 1892 the three clubs who subscribed for the Cup which replaced the Belt, Prestwick, the R. and A., and the Honourable Company, promoted the events in turn. In 1893 Royal St George's and Royal Liverpool joined in a five-year cycle, and in 1909 the Royal Cinque Ports Club at Deal was added. For the next five years those six clubs constituted an unofficial championship committee, but it was a loose alliance because each championship was managed entirely by the home club with the other five having little or no control over the local arrangements. This naturally created differences in the nature and scale of the different promotions. The greatest enterprise was shown at St Andrews, because there the town had a vested interest in the welfare of the Old Course, and it was a public arena. But conservatism was rife at the other clubs, and no one concerned with the national championships then or for many years afterwards could escape the impression that while the 'championship clubs' were jealous of the honour attached to that description, most of them tended to regard the affair as one to which the public would be admitted almost by grace and favour, and which must not be allowed to interfere with the comfort and privileges of the members.

The Amateur Championship followed a similar line in development although, since more clubs were involved in the management, the host club had less freedom of action. Following the successful promotion of an unofficial Amateur Championship in 1885 by the Liverpool club, the event was put on an official basis in the following year by twenty-three clubs subscribing for a Challenge Cup. Three other clubs joined in later years but, although twenty-six courses were represented on this 'committee of management', the championship was a quarter of a century old before it was played on any links other than St Andrews, Prestwick, Muirfield, Hoylake and Sandwich. After the Great War, which affected life in so many ways and did not spare golf from the wind of change, there was a general feeling that important affairs like championships should be controlled by some central authority. The clubs most concerned were no longer able to provide all the voluntary labour required or shoulder the steadily increasing costs. In December 1919, delegates of the promoting clubs meeting in Edinburgh accepted a proposal by the Honourable Company that in the interests of golf there should be a supreme ruling authority and that the Royal and Ancient Golf Club be asked to accept management of the two championships and custody of the cups. St Andrews was invested with full authority for the first time, but the Edinburgh meeting aroused no general interest, and for many years afterwards there was no great change in the running of the championships. Most of the preparatory work was still done by the host clubs in turn, and another World War was over before the R. and A. Championship Committee assumed full control over each promotion.

The two championships, the Boys' Championship, the Walker Cup matches and other big international contests make a full programme for the Championship Committee and the R. and A.

secretariat, and the arrangements are satisfactory in all respects. There have been many critics resenting the archaic situation whereby golf politics and the control of the game are in the hands of members of a private club. But in 1919 no one questioned the fitness of the R. and A. to be the ruling body of British golf, and today dissident voices are few.

One reason why the overlordship of the R. and A. is accepted so placidly is that most aspects of golf in Britain are controlled, for all practical purposes, by separate bodies enjoying autonomy in their own fields. The Ladies' Golf Union governs women's golf through national associations; the men have similar bodies in the four home countries; the Professional Golfers' Association administers its affairs through eight district sections; and every department of club life has its representative body. The control of the Standard Scratch Score and Handicapping Scheme is vested in the Council of the Golf Unions; and the R. and A. has supreme authority in only two matters—the rules and their enforcement, and the promotion of major championships and international matches. Even in these fields the R. and A. can and does seek the advice and opinions of outside organizations and individuals. The government of golf, therefore, is not an authoritarian affair directed from a citadel in St Andrews, but a conglomeration of interests all working from their various standpoints towards the same end—orderly progress of golf to greater prestige and power.

CHAPTER 30

Present and future

Golf was a purely Scottish game for so many centuries that its world-wide expansion in the last hundred years can only be described as phenomenal. In Britain alone, it is estimated, $1\frac{1}{2}$ million men, women and children play, and millions more have become acquainted with golf through newspaper, radio and television coverage of big events. More than six millions play in the United States where, as in most other countries, there is an insatiable demand for adequate facilities. Golf has a flourishing and growing industry, and millions in a dozen different currencies are poured into it by all classes from dukes to dustmen. This comparison has a literal foundation, for dukes and other noblemen have been associated with golf throughout its history, and when a Manchester householder recently dumped a bag of old clubs for the dustmen to cart away he fathered what must be one of the world's strangest courses—six holes averaging 80 yards in length, laid out on an acre of waste ground at the municipal rubbish depot!

Much wealth is spent on the construction of luxury courses and buildings in exotic surroundings, but the future of golf does not depend on the projects of affluent people who are already golfers. It rests on the feasibility of supplying enough playing space for the ever-growing army of humbler players, so that awakening enthusiasm is not stifled at birth. Yet even the non-affluent beginner requires modern facilities and these, even in the simplest forms, demand money and space. The days of free golf along the seashore with nature as the only green-keeper belong to the distant past. The present-day course requires upwards of 100 acres of enclosed land, the construction of eighteen greens and at least twice that number of teeing-grounds, the excavation of bunkers, the purchase of sand, seed, fertilizers and machinery, the recruiting of staff, and the building of accommodation. Land is getting scarcer and dearer, the cost of labour and materials is soaring, and the purchasing power of money diminishing. A simple and modest project for a full-length course in Britain would cost about £100,000, and might well cost twice as much in ten or fifteen years' time.

The figures for various 1974–5 municipal projects, quoted in an earlier chapter, show that costs rise partly by the shortage and consequently high price of suburban land, partly by the fact that municipalities are spending public money, and partly by the need in many cases to make provision for other recreations. In the private sector British ideas of golf course finance are indeed modest, and most of the country's leading architects spend a lot of time abroad designing and planning the lay-out of prestigious courses incorporating luxury real-estate developments. Nevertheless, there have been several projects in Britain which compare with more costly ventures overseas, and in 1974 an entirely new departure was made when trustees of the Duke of Bedford's estate at Woburn launched a scheme for two full-length courses on 300 acres of land, and looked for outside help to meet the cost. It was proposed to raise £600,000 by inviting wealthy golfers in the neighbourhood to take up founder-member bonds of £5,000 each, and Charles Lawrie, former Walker Cup captain, was brought in as architect to plan a championship course of 7,015 yards and a shorter course of 6,645 yards.

A scheme of this kind makes little or no contribution to the root problem of too many golfers chasing too few courses. All the golfers responding to the Woburn appeal would be almost certainly members of existing clubs, and their ability to finance the deal to the extent of £5,000 each would make them automatically members of a privileged circle. The Woburn scheme adds two courses to the number in Britain but does nothing to help the homeless golfer.

Of equal importance with the shortage of courses is the shortage of men to look after them. The British Golf Greenkeepers' Association has had an apprentice training scheme running for about ten years at an average annual output of seventeen trained men. This has been done with no outside help, not even from the clubs who benefit from the operation. On the other hand, clubs are continually on the hunt for well-trained and experienced greenkeepers, and expect to get them and their know-how for unrealistic rewards. When, years ago, the R. and A. appointed two ex-caddies to look after the Old Course at St Andrews at a joint wage of £6 per annum, the job required no special knowledge and no tools beyond the gardening implements of the time. Nowadays the greenkeeper is expected to know all about the production, care and treatment of turf, the handling and maintenance of expensive machinery, and the control of staff in an economical way. To gain his knowledge he attends training courses at the Sports Turf Research Institute, listens to lectures on various turf topics, and carries out his own experiments at home. And his reward? As a young man completing his three years' apprenticeship under the BGGA scheme he will be offered about £20 a week, sometimes less; and if he stays in the business he might hope eventually to become assistant greenkeeper at about £30 a week, or even head greenkeeper, a post which can, but all too seldom does, attract a top salary of £2,500. But even less exalted head greenkeepers, those earning less than £2,000 a year, are constantly under the scrutiny of members who are not slow to complain if the course is in less than perfect condition. The same members are equally ready to complain about the cost of running the club, and loathe to suffer subscription increases which the situation demands.

In its basic elements golf is not expensive for the individual. The beginner can spend as much as he can afford, and the millionaire as much as he desires, for the game remains the same whatever the scale of expenditure. Many golfers lay out £150 on full equipment and pay an average annual subscription of £50, although membership of some exclusive clubs costs very much more. On the other hand enjoyment can be obtained—some will say more genuine enjoyment—from the use of modest equipment on a public course. But in both cases the golfer requires playing facilities, and so far in the last twenty-five years the supply of new courses has failed to match the demand. Here again, except in opulent circles and holiday developments abroad, the question of finance is critical.

In this respect Britain is one of the poor relations. For many years the United States was top of the league in the money per player spent on golf, but Japan seems likely to surpass all previous records. Many of the new courses constructed or planned in Japan since the Second World War have cost at least a million pounds each, and some considerably more. In Italy, Spain, Portugal and the holiday islands of the Mediterranean it is not unusual for a quarter of a million or more to be expended on courses which, while designed primarily as playgrounds for holiday-makers and permanent residents, are mostly full-length lay-outs on which championships can be played.

A few ambitious and therefore costly projects have been carried out by syndicates or individuals in Britain, but most of the courses being made in this country are on fairly modest lines, because private purses are limited and municipal and other public under-takings are accountable to ratepayers or shareholders. Local government bodies can now maintain, in the light of experience in other localities, that the use of public money for golf is justified. The capital expenditure may be heavy but the course itself becomes an asset, particularly if included with other sports in a recreational centre.

The expansion of the 1890s was due to the rapid formation of private clubs by golfers who required seclusion from the public. But it is probable that further significant growth can take place only at the expense of private clubs. Some will be in danger of acquisition by local authorities; others will be forced by financial pressures to open their doors to everyone. Most of the 1,700 private clubs are not in real danger, and many are important enough or rich enough to remain independent. But the shadow hovering over the private club is that of crowds of newcomers clamouring for playing-space.

It is paradoxical that organizations like Golf Foundation and the Central Council for Physical Recreation are working hard to ensure a steady increase in the number of players, while the pro-vision of facilities, despite the equally hard efforts of the Golf Development Council, lags behind demand. Apart from the mass tuition classes run by Golf Foundation, several county school golf associations have been formed to stage competitions and play inter-county matches. Another important development has been the establishment of a coaching award for school-teachers, who thereby become qualified to teach the basic principles of golf. That move has the full blessing of the Professional Golfers' Association for obvious reasons, since it will help to deliver rough-hewn raw material into the hands of the professional instructors. The PGA's own scheme for training and qualifying assistant professionals in all aspects of the craft is another important contribution to the orderly future of golf. Players of the present generation have every incentive and plenty of opportunities for becoming proficient, and in that respect are more fortunate than were their grandfathers. Even fifty years ago, young golfers who had been properly coached by a professional were in the minority, and as a result many golfers grew up with faults which could not be eradicated in maturity and permanently barred them from full achievement.

Half a century ago most professionals started as assistants on leaving school, and were too involved in the work of the shop to spare much time for the development of their playing skills. Nowadays the tendency is for a promising youngster to play as an amateur during his teens and prove himself in junior golf or even, precociously, in senior golf before deciding to turn professional. In that case he enters the professional world as a competent player hoping to concentrate on winning prize money to the exclusion of everything else. The PGA training scheme is intended to prepare youngsters for the business of being club professionals; so that, if their hopes of becoming tournament stars are not fulfilled, as indeed they will not be in the majority of cases, they will have an alternative occupation and a settled livelihood. For many years now, hundreds of youngsters have entered professional golf with eyes fixed on the glittering prizes, only to endure season after season of failure and frustration and be compelled to drop out of the race without having any solid ground on which to rest.

In various ways the PGA and the other bodies mentioned are united in the aim to make the best use of material, and nothing more clearly shows the advance of wise thinking over recent years than the willingness of individuals and organizations to get round the table and shape policies in accord. Even forty years ago this would not have been possible, and the universal co-operation now practised is the best insurance against any attempt to upset the structure of golf and the nature of its government in Britain. The Royal and Ancient Golf Club of St Andrews has never before been so firmly established as the ruling body of British golf, and this is due not to any diminution in the democratic feelings of golfers, but to the fact that the R. and A., in many ways, has moved with the times and put tradition in the background.

There are some critics of the constitution of British golf who ask why the members of a private club at their twice-yearly business meetings should have the power to vote on proposals affecting the future of millions of players in these islands and in many countries overseas.

In practice, of course, any decisions affecting all golfers are not taken without full discussion with ruling and advisory bodies at home and abroad, and proper ventilation in the Press. The power of the R. and A. indeed is inherent in its constitution. At the period when it was given complete control over the rules, in 1897, it was a members' club in no way different from Prestwick, the Honourable Company, Royal Liverpool or any of the principal clubs. By 1919, when control of the championships was relinquished by the consortium of clubs, the R. and A. had become an international organization. Today the premier club has a maximum of 1,750 members, 700 of whom must be resident overseas, and these 700 are spread over forty-five countries. Altogether fifty-two countries are affiliated to the R. and A. through their national bodies, together with such comprehensive associations as the Ladies' Golf Union, the European Golf Association, the South American Golf Federation and the Asia Golf Federation.

In the present golf government in Britain can be seen, less distinctly but still visible, the thread of centuries-old class autocracy. Two hundred years ago the Honourable Company and the St Andrews Society made rules and no one challenged their right to do so. They dictated how golf should be played and humbler clubs and players fell into line for a time. But later there were several rebellions against any form of central government, and golf clubs in various parts of the country, considering themselves equal in standing to the R. and A., were supreme in their own domains. They were the bold haughty barons of nineteenth-century golf unwilling to acknowledge a superior authority. Eventually they all submitted to the rule of St Andrews, which has not been questioned for more than half a century. No one knows what the next fifty years will produce. It is possible that if, in the 1890s, Dr Laidlaw Purves had succeeded in forming a Golf Association for men, such an organization might have been accepted, in the fluid circumstances of those days, as a ruling body on the lines of the United States Golf Association. But the moment passed, the chance was missed, and the long progress towards R. and A. supremacy, begun nearly a hundred years earlier, ended in the establishment of the seat of government at St Andrews.

It is strange, in an age of protest, intolerance of authority, and rebellion against restrictions, that this situation should continue apparently to the general satisfaction. The R. and A. pronounces on the laws of the game, runs championships and reaches decisions on many important matters without raising a yelp of protest from the fairways. But that is typical of British life generally and British golf in particular. The average player, intent on pursuing the little white ball over the springy turf in the open air, has neither the time nor the inclination to worry about the politics of the game. He is content with golf as it is.

Bibliography

FARNIE, H. B. (1857), *The Golfer's Annual, By 'A Keen Hand'*, Whitehead & Orr. The earliest comprehensive textbook, covering every aspect of the game from its early history to a discussion of its philosophy, with plenty of instructional hints in between.

CLARK, R. R. (1875), *Golf: a Royal and Ancient Game*, Clark. Mainly historical, and chiefly remarkable for the many extracts from the minutes of the earliest golf clubs, and interesting biographical sketches.

SIMPSON, W. G. (1887), *The Art of Golf*, Hamilton.

STEWART, J. L., ed. (1887), *Golfiana Miscellanea*, Hamilton.

HUTCHINSON, H. G., ed. (1890), *Golf* (The Badminton Library), Longmans, Green. Historical and biographical, with instruction, contributed by several authors.

FITTIS, R. S. (1891), *Sports and Pastimes of Scotland*, Gardner.

HUTCHINSON, H. G. (1891), *Famous Golf Links*, Longmans, Green.

MCPHERSON, J. G. (1891), *Golf and Golfers Past and Present*, Blackwood.

CLAPCOTT, C. B. (1895), *The Rules of the Ten Oldest Golf Clubs*, Edinburgh. Including some historical sketches.

PARK, W., Jnr (1896), *The Game of Golf*, Longmans, Green. The first book produced by a professional golfer, including not only history and instruction, but also technical information on course construction and upkeep.

MCBAIN, J. and FERNIE, W. (1897), *Golf*, Dean.

HUTCHINSON, H. G. (1899), *The Book of Golf and Golfers*, Longmans, Green. The mixture as before.

TAYLOR, J. H. (1902), *On Golf: Impressions, Comments and Hints,* Hutchinson.

HEZLET, M. (1904), *Ladies' Golf,* Hutchinson.

VARDON, H. (1905), *The Complete Golfer,* Methuen.

COLVILLE, J. (1907), *The Glasgow Golf Club,* Smith. Including much interesting material about golf and golfers in the late eighteenth and early nineteenth centuries.

LEACH, H., ed. (1907), *Great Golfers in the Making,* Methuen. Autobiographic sketches of most of the leading golfers of the previous half-century, amateur and professional.

HUTCHINSON, H. G. (1919), *Fifty Years of Golf,* Newnes.

KIRKALDY, A. (1921), *Fifty Years of Golf: My Memories,* Fisher Unwin.

STRINGER, M. E. (1924), *Golfing Reminiscences,* Mills & Boon. Autobiography tracing the development of women's golf from the 1890s.

BENNETT, A. (1943), *The St Andrews Golf Club Centenary,* privately published. Much interesting information about early artisan players and professionals at St Andrews.

TAYLOR, J. H. (1943), *Golf my Life's Work,* Cape. An autobiography covering the early days of many developments—artisans, public courses, the PGA.

DARWIN, B. (1944), *Golf Between Two Wars,* Chatto & Windus.

MORAN, F. (1946), *Golfers Gallery,* Oliver & Boyd.

PREEDY, A. (1950), 'Home Park Golf Club from Birth to Jubilee' (typescript). Intimate insight into life in a typical suburban club in the 1890s.

VARIOUS (1952), *A History of Golf in Britain,* Cassel. Distinguished contributors covering the game, its implements and its players over the centuries.

BROWNING, R. (1955), *A History of Golf,* Dent. A shorter history of special interest for research into the supposed origins of the game.

COUSINS, G. (1958), *Golfers at Law,* Stanley Paul. A complete history of the rules.

VARIOUS (1960), *A History of Sandy Lodge Golf Club,* privately published.

GOLF FOUNDATION LTD (1963), *Making Room for Golf*. An exposition of the problem of providing adequate playing facilities, with notes on procedure.

GOODBAN, J. W. D., ed. (1964), *The Royal North Devon Golf Club (A Centenary Anthology)*, privately published.

SCUDAMORE, E. (1965), *The Early Days of Golf at Wimbledon*, privately published.

COUSINS, G. and SCOTT, T. (1971), *A Century of Opens*, Muller. Accounts of great championships and biographical references to great champions.

POTTINGER, G. (1972), *Muirfield and the Honourable Company*, Scottish Academic Press.

Index of clubs, links and courses

General index

DATE		

THE BAKER & TAYLOR CO.